PLEASE
RECEIP
S0-AAB-453

JANE AUSTEN

Introductions and Interventions

JANE AUSTEN

Introductions and Interventions

JOHN WILTSHIRE

Macquarie
Regional Library

© *John Wiltshire, 2003, 2006*

All rights reserved. No reproduction, copy or transmission of this publication may be made without written permission.

No paragraph of this publication may be reproduced, copied or transmitted save with written permission or in accordance with the provisions of the Copyright, Designs and Patents Act 1988, or under the terms of any licence permitting limited copying issued by the Copyright Licensing Agency, 90 Tottenham Court Road, London W1T 4LP.

Any person who does any unauthorised act in relation to this publication may be liable to criminal prosecution and civil claims for damages.

The author has asserted his right to be identified as the author of this work in accordance with the Copyright, Designs and Patents Act 1988.

Originally published 2003 by Macmillan India
This edition published 2006 by
PALGRAVE MACMILLAN
Houndmills, Basingstoke, Hampshire RG21 6XS and
175 Fifth Avenue, New York, N.Y. 10010
Published by arrangement with
Macmillan India Ltd
2/10 Ansari Road, New Delhi 110 002
Companies and representatives throughout the world

PALGRAVE MACMILLAN is the global academic imprint of the Palgrave Macmillan division of St. Martin's Press, LLC and of Palgrave Macmillan Ltd. Macmillan® is a registered trademark in the United States, United Kingdom and other countries. Palgrave is a registered trademark in the European Union and other countries.

ISBN-13: 978–0–230–00749–9   hardback
ISBN-10: 0–230–00749–X   hardback

ISBN-13: 978–0–230–00750–5   paperback
ISBN-10: 0–230–00750–3   paperback

A catalogue record for this book is available from the British Library.

A catalog record for this book is available from the Library of Congress.

10   9   8   7   6   5   4   3   2   1
15 14 13 12 11 10 09 08 07 06

Printed and bound in India at Sanat Printers

This edition is not for sale in India, Pakistan, Bangladesh and Nepal

For
Marie, Roseann and Helen

Contents

Preface

This book consists of essays on Jane Austen originally written over the last decade or so for a range of publications and audiences, newly revised for this volume. I have called them Introductions and Interventions to mark their different styles. The first are essays on Jane Austen's novels *Pride and Prejudice, Mansfield Park, Emma* and *Persuasion,* which, without engaging in critical controversy, introduce readers to some of the key features, including the narrative artistry, of these four major texts. The second consists of articles, addressed to readers already familiar with these texts, of a more original and interventionary nature—essays which take up issues in the past and current criticism of Jane Austen.

Austen is a writer whose novels, some more obviously than others, invite, even require, re-reading. In the structure of this book I hope to accompany the reader through the experience of first acquaintance with Austen's work, followed up by a more informed and sophisticated understanding. The final essay, especially written for this volume, explores the attraction of Jane Austen for readers outside England in the contemporary world.

In all of the essays the page references are to the volumes in the currently most commonly cited edition, that of R.W. Chapman, *The Oxford Illustrated Jane Austen,* first published in 1923, and many times reprinted, which reproduces the volume divisions sometimes ignored by other editors. The first reference in each chapter gives the standard abbreviation (*P&P, MP, E, P*): subsequent citations just give the page number.

Earlier versions of Chapters 2, 3 and 4 were originally published in *The Cambridge Companion to Jane Austen* edited by Edward Copeland and Juliet McMaster; an earlier version of Chapter 5 in *Persuasions*, 23, 2001; Chapter 6 first appeared in *The Cambridge Quarterly*; Chapters 8 and 9 are based on essays written for *Approaches to Teaching* Emma, edited by Marcia McKlintock Folsom, Modern Language Association (forthcoming).

1

Pride and Prejudice

Jane Austen first wrote the novel that became *Pride and Prejudice* under the title 'First Impressions' between 1796 and 1797. Over the next decade she revised and rewrote it, lopping and cropping it, as she writes in a letter of January 1813 when she received her first copy of the novel. In that letter to her sister, Jane Austen also says 'I must confess that I think [Elizabeth Bennet] as delightful a creature as ever appeared in print', and readers for nearly two hundred years have agreed with her. But partly because of its distance from us in time, modern readers unused to Jane Austen's work will probably have some initial difficulties in approaching her 'world'.

When *Pride and Prejudice* was first published it appeared in three volumes. Although these volume divisions are omitted in many modern editions of the novel, they are important to understanding the novel's structure. Volume I, which consists of the first twenty-three chapters, is set entirely in Longbourn, and though it introduces Elizabeth to both Wickham and Darcy and includes Mr Collins's proposal, ends with the removal of the Bingley party to London and Mr Collins's acceptance by Charlotte. In Volume II the perspective widens as Elizabeth visits Jane and her aunt in London and then Charlotte at Hunsford, making the acquaintance of Lady Catherine de Bourgh at Rosings Park. This volume includes Mr Darcy's proposal and Elizabeth's refusal. In its last few chapters

Elizabeth seems back where she started, confined to the small world of Longbourn again, but it ends with the Gardiners' invitation to visit Derbyshire and the words 'To Pemberley, therefore, they were to go' (*P&P* 241). Thus we can see that the original volume divisions, in this novel as in the later ones, are important. They structure and pace the narrative. Volume III opens with Elizabeth away from home, and with the scene at Pemberley that marks both Elizabeth's and Darcy's change of heart. The broadening of horizons in the novel thus corresponds exactly to the broadening of Elizabeth's personal horizons, which is an important aspect of the novel's subject.

The first two volumes both end with a chapter that reflects severely upon Elizabeth Bennet's family: each emphasizes how much her prospects, both literally and figuratively, depend upon them. And this is because of the importance of her status as a gentlewoman.

A GENTLEMAN'S DAUGHTER

It is best to approach the question of Jane Austen's world—the ways it strikingly differs from and the ways it resembles our own—through a careful reading of *Pride and Prejudice* itself. For the novel is not simply a portrait of a society, nor does it use that society simply as the background setting for a romantic love story (in the manner of many other later novelists, and even some of the films based on Austen's work). Essentially *Pride and Prejudice* is an argument about civil society and the love story is an essential part of the argument. 'He is a gentleman. I am a gentleman's daughter', Elizabeth Bennet cries at the height of her confrontation with Lady Catherine de Bourgh in Volume III, Chapter 14 (Chapter 56 in many modern editions). Clearly, the question of whether one is, or is not, a gentleman or a gentleman's daughter is of some importance in the novel.

A 'gentleman' can be roughly defined as a man who does not earn his living directly, who lives on the income derived from property, usually held in the form of land, but sometimes in stocks and shares, and thus indirectly in manufacturing industry. Clergymen of the Church of England were also commonly held to be gentlemen, as were commissioned officers in the army. But this is only a rough working definition because it is an important part of the book's argument that being a gentleman (or a lady) depends on more than just one's place in the social hierarchy or on one's income. Elizabeth's uncle Mr Gardiner would not be considered a 'gentleman' by the definition just given, for he is 'in trade' and earns his income directly, yet he is called a gentleman and it is an important part of Darcy's development to realize that indeed he is one.

Lady Catherine de Bourgh is unimpeachably a lady, having a title and a great income and estate, but is she really a lady in her behaviour to others? Darcy, too, has a great estate, but this does not prevent Elizabeth Bennet, when she rejects his proposal, from commenting sharply on his ungentleman-like manner. It is a blow that goes home. Like many writers in the eighteenth century Jane Austen is engaged in the project to moralise the term 'gentleman'. Steele, for example writing in *The Tatler*, early in the century (about 1710) wrote that 'The Appellation of Gentleman is never to be affixed to a man's Circumstances, but to his Behaviour in them.' Jane Austen is suggesting, as she does on many occasions throughout the novel, that the term gentleman is not and should not be tied to a particular social category: it is for her an honorific title, earned through the possession of personal qualities. It is Darcy's 'arrogance, . . . conceit, and . . . selfish disdain of the feelings of others' (193) that calls forth Elizabeth's rebuke. Throughout the novel then, the social and ethical meanings of the term gentleman are held in tension. Very much the same thing can be said about the associated word 'pride'.

Jane Austen uses language very precisely, with an acute awareness of the various possibilities in many key words, but another initial hurdle is its comparative formality, and beginning readers may tend to associate formality with officialese and politeness. An examination of the scene of Darcy's proposal, which occurs in Volume II, Chapter 11, is a useful corrective to this assumption. A reading aloud is all that is needed. Both speakers are polite, in a sense (they certainly do not swear, for instance). But the formal structure of their sentences cannot disguise the fury and the indignation they both feel; the more furious they are, the more biting and decisive is their expression.

Another point to note is that although *Pride and Prejudice* is certainly a novel of conversations rather than actions, most of the conversations are arguments. And, though they are conducted in the form of general discussion, they concern matters in which the private stake of the participants is great. The conversation between Elizabeth and Jane in the first chapter of the second volume, for instance, covers such topics as the inconsistency of human character, the relationship between appearance and reality, whether hurtful behaviour is usually the result of design, and so on, and it is conducted in the terms of logical argument ('Your first position is false', says Elizabeth). But underlying and shaping the discussion are intense personal interests and feelings. Jane's happiness has been jeopardized by Bingley's abrupt departure; Elizabeth has been deceived by her best friend. Another scene whose apparent formality certainly does not moderate or mask the intensity of the feelings involved—in this case mutual anger— is Lady Catherine de Bourgh's visit to Longbourn. Elizabeth never exceeds the bounds of politeness, but she speaks with a forthrightness and vigour that is unmistakable.

Darcy, Elizabeth believes, before she has read his letter, has the 'worst kind of pride'—that which is affronted by the lack of 'importance' (meaning wealth and wealthy relations) in Jane Bennet's family. There might be another, and, it is implied, more justifiable, pride, which was offended by their 'want of sense'. Pride, it is evident, has many varieties. For the reader's amusement Jane Austen puts an abstract discussion of the varieties of pride into the mouth of Mary Bennet in Chapter 5, early in the novel; but there is also a more intelligent exchange about pride between Elizabeth and Darcy in Chapter 12. 'Indeed he has no improper pride', Elizabeth cries in defence of Darcy to her father near the conclusion of the novel. But by this time she has learned what Darcy intended when in their earlier exchange he had claimed, 'where there is real superiority of mind, pride will always be under good regulation'. She adds, 'He is perfectly amiable.' What is true of the word gentleman in *Pride and Prejudice* is true also of the words pride and amiable, and of many of the key terms of the novelist's language. They are not fixed but fluid in their meanings; the meaning of a word varies startlingly with the context and according to who uses it.

So the reader of Jane Austen is continually invited to notice how a word is being used and to assess whether it is being used justifiably, sloppily or mischievously. 'Amiable', for instance, is initially what Wickham obviously is, and Darcy obviously is not; and the novelist asks the reader to assess what quality it is that this word denotes, and to decide upon its value. She uses it herself continually in different ways: at the opening of Volume II, Chapter 2, for instance, Mr Collins is thinking of 'his amiable Charlotte' and in the next paragraph we are told that Mrs Gardiner 'was an amiable, intelligent, elegant woman'. Does the word carry the same implication in each instance? Other key words of this kind are 'sensible' ('Can he be a sensible man, sir?' Elizabeth asks her father when Mr Collins's letter is read aloud, but Mrs Bennet commends him for speaking so 'sensibly') and 'elegant'.

It is a useful practice to underline and note these recurrent words where they occur and to consider how they are used on different occasions. If you do this, you find that many of the novel's most important words are adjectives or adverbs that have to do with manners. Mr Wickham's amiability is very much a matter of his 'agreeable' manners—'whatever he said was said well, whatever he did was done gracefully'. Such important words are elegant, prudent, or imprudent, impertinent, and especially proper and improper, and associated nouns such as decorum and impropriety. Since these words are no longer used much in assessing people's behaviour it may be difficult for the reader to understand at first what they denote and their importance. A crucial example is Elizabeth's reflections on her father and mother at the end of the second volume:

Elizabeth, however, had never been blind to the impropriety of her father's behaviour as a husband. She had always seen it with pain; but respecting his abilities, and grateful for his affectionate treatment of herself, she endeavoured to forget what she could not overlook, and to banish from her thoughts that continual breach of connubial obligation and decorum which, in exposing his wife to the contempt of her own children, was so highly reprehensible. But she had never felt so strongly as now the disadvantages which must attend the children of so unsuitable a marriage. . . . (236)

There are two distinct charges here, though the words impropriety and decorum blend them. Mr Bennet's continual ironic and contemptuous treatment of his wife exposes her to her own children's ridicule; and it also places those children at a social disadvantage. Most modern readers are apt to be much more sympathetic to the first meaning than to the second, which is what the words impropriety and decorum imply.

To be able to sympathize with this charge, one needs to take account of two things: first, the importance the 'connections' of a person have in this society, and second, the significance, in Jane Austen's view, of manners. What Darcy in his proposal speech to Elizabeth calls 'the inferiority of your connections' does not refer, as his letter makes clear, to their lack of comparable wealth or status, but to their 'total want of propriety' (198). 'Connections' means here not just the immediate family of the heroine, but more distant relations: the fact that one of Elizabeth's uncles is an attorney and the other in trade—neither of them positions comfortably within the genteel class. Elizabeth Bennet is not simply an individual, separate from her family: as an unmarried woman particularly she is to an extent at the mercy of her family, whose behaviour, in the eyes of the world, justly, or unjustly, affects her own status and character.

Throughout the novel, to take up the second point, Jane Austen assumes a close association between personal qualities and social manners. The impropriety of Mr and Mrs Bennet's different behaviours is not simply their bad manners—their failure to obey some arbitrary code of genteel conduct; it is, so the novelist suggests, the outward form of a real personal deficiency. The word 'suggests' is used because while Jane Austen sometimes argues or shows, at other times she perhaps merely assumes the direct connection between improper behaviour and egoism or conceit. Impropriety is sometimes rudeness in the obvious sense, for instance when Lady Catherine demands to know what her nephew is telling Miss Bennet (173) and asks Elizabeth her age (166). But artificial or over-elaborate courtesies and flatteries are equally felt to be embarrassing and improper. There is no difficulty in connecting Mr Collins's obsequiousness and artificial language with his self-importance and stupidity, but on the other hand Sir William Lucas is the butt of comic ridicule merely for his elaborate and extravagant courtesy.

The scene of the Netherfield ball is the crucial one here (Volume I, Chapter 18). 'To Elizabeth it appeared, that had her family made an agreement to expose themselves as much as they could during the evening, it would have been impossible for them to play their parts with more spirit, or finer success . . .' (101). She is intensely mortified and ashamed as first Mr Collins, then her mother and then her sister Mary and her father display their lack of tact. Her shame certainly comes about because she participates, by proxy, in the reactions of the Bingley sisters and Darcy, but it is also because she perceives that Mr Collins's pomposity is a sign of his conceit, that her mother's bragging of her daughter's expected marriage to a rich man is a sign of her ambitiousness and snobbery, and that Mary's bad singing is compounded by her complete lack of self-awareness and by her sharing in her mother's desire to push herself forward. (There is a deeper level to this shame, explored in Chapter 5 of this book.) But the question of how far the accusation of impropriety rests ultimately on personal failings—egoism, conceit and the like—and how far on failure to observe the demands of a social code which we may no longer share, will be answered differently by each reader. A good passage to take as a subject for this discussion, and one that resembles the scene of the Netherfield ball, is Mrs Bennet's visit to Netherfield while Jane is ill (Volume I, Chapter 9).

PREJUDICE

Elizabeth may be clear-sighted about her family, but she is certainly much less so about herself, about Darcy and Wickham and her closest friend, Charlotte Lucas. The conversation at Netherfield alluded to in the previous paragraph is concerned with knowing people, with the study of human nature and with 'intricate characters'. Much of *Pride and Prejudice* is concerned with these questions: how much do we know of the people about us, and how do we really come to know them? Elizabeth is shocked by Charlotte's acceptance of Mr Collins, but the reader has been given warning signs in the preceding chapters. In her remarks about Darcy in Chapter 5, and in her discussion with Elizabeth about marriage in Chapter 6 ('Happiness in marriage is entirely a matter of chance . . . it is better to know as little as possible of the defects of the person with whom you are to pass your life,' says Charlotte), she reveals a worldliness and cynicism that, as Elizabeth laughingly declares, is 'not sound'. And, with the benefit of hindsight, one may find something suspicious in Charlotte's apparent friendliness to Elizabeth at the Netherfield ball: 'She owed her greatest relief to her friend Miss Lucas, who often joined them, and goodnaturedly engaged Mr Collins's conversation to herself' (102). Then there is the moment at the end of Chapter 21 where Charlotte deliberately stays about so that she can overhear what Mr Collins says about his proposal to Mrs Bennet. Charlotte may be scheming, and then again she may not.

What happens with Charlotte happens also with Wickham, and in a much more important and complex way, with Darcy. Charlotte's remarks and behaviour do not necessarily mean that she has her sights already set on marriage with Mr Collins; Elizabeth's refusal to believe what she says is attractive and justifiable in its context, and the reader, what is more, shares Elizabeth's responses. The important thing is to avoid interpreting the novel 'backwards', that is to say, reading the characters' speech and behaviour through knowledge of their ultimate outcomes. If we do this, the danger is that we find ourselves in an artificial position of superiority to Elizabeth Bennet, through whose eyes most, though not quite all, of the action of the novel is seen. And her understandings make perfect sense whilst we are reading.

So when Elizabeth engages in conversational duelling with Darcy, the reader naturally takes her side. We hear Darcy's remarks as Elizabeth hears them. It is only later, and on turning back to their dialogues, that we see his remarks have potentialities of meaning that Elizabeth misses. The critic Reuben Brower remarked on Jane Austen's 'awareness that the same remark or action has very different meaning in different relations'. Part of the achievement of *Pride and Prejudice* is to make the reader realize, he wrote, 'that it is difficult to know any complex person, that knowledge of a man like Darcy is an interpretation and a construction, not a simple absolute'. A discussion of the exchange between Elizabeth and Darcy in Chapter 11 illustrates this:

'Mr Darcy is not to be laughed at!' cried Elizabeth. 'That is an uncommon advantage and uncommon I hope it will continue, for it would be a great loss to me to have many such acquaintance. I dearly love a laugh.'

'Miss Bingley,' said he, 'has given me credit for more than can be. The wisest and the best of men, nay, the wisest and best of their actions, may be rendered ridiculous by a person whose first object in life is a joke.'

'Certainly', replied Elizabeth—'there are such people, but I hope I am not one of *them*. I hope I never ridicule what is wise or good. Follies and nonsense, whims and inconsistencies do divert me, I own, and I laugh at them whenever I can.—But these, I suppose are precisely what you are without.'

'Perhaps that is not possible for any one. But it has been the study of my life to avoid those weaknesses which often expose a strong understanding to ridicule.'

'Such as vanity and pride.'

'Yes, vanity is a weakness indeed. But pride—where there is a real superiority of mind, pride will be always under good regulation.'

Elizabeth turned away to hide a smile.

'Your examination of Mr Darcy is over, I presume,' said Miss Bingley;—'and pray ~ what is the result?'

'I am perfectly convinced by it that Mr Darcy has no defect. He owns it himself without disguise.'

'No'—said Darcy, 'I have made no such pretension. I have faults enough, but they are not, I hope, of understanding. My temper I dare not vouch for.—It is I believe too little yielding—certainly too little for the convenience of the world. I cannot forget the follies ~ , and vices of others as soon as I ought, nor their offences against myself. My feelings are ~ not puffed about with every attempt to move them. My temper would perhaps be called resentful. —My good opinion once lost is lost for ever.'

'*That* is a failing indeed!'—cried Elizabeth. 'Implacable resentment is a shade in a character. But you have chosen your fault well.—I really cannot *laugh* at it. You are safe from me.'

'There is, I believe, in every disposition a tendency to some particular evil, a natural defect, which not even the best education can overcome.'

'And your defect is a propensity to hate every body.'

'And yours' he replied with a smile, 'is to wilfully to misunderstand them.'

'Do let us have a little music,'—cried Miss Bingley, tired of a conversation in which she had no share. (57–8)

In the above passage the words 'Your defect is wilfully to misunderstand them' alerts us to the fact that Elizabeth's lively responses miss something that Darcy intends by his speeches. They can justifiably be read in two ways—either as humourless, arrogant and self-important, or as genuine attempts at self-knowledge, rather inhibited by pride. Darcy may be seizing the opportunity of having, for once, the chance to pursue a serious conversation with a lively and intelligent listener, an opportunity he certainly has not had with the Hursts or Miss Bingley. But Elizabeth persists in taking them only as humourless, arrogant and self-important.

Elizabeth's refusal to be serious, in Darcy's sense, is what stimulates his self-examination. And his speeches can be read as either boastful or self-critical because they are actually both. The hesitations and repetitions of Darcy's longest speech about himself suggest how confession and pride are mingled together. If the reader is in doubt as to how to take the speech, that is because Darcy himself does not know what he intends by it, where the final stress is to go. How the speech is read (or heard) determines what is made of Elizabeth's accusation of 'implacable resentment'. This is either an appropriately severe response to an 'indirect boast' (to use the term Darcy himself uses about Bingley), or a delighted seizing of the chance to snatch victory out of defeat in this conversational crossing of swords.

Because Darcy's speech is both supercilious and honest, Elizabeth's response to it is simultaneously accurate and mistaken. It is when Darcy says that she wilfully misunderstands him that it can be seen most plainly how her refusal to flatter him has stimulated him to interpret his own intentions. His usual companions conspire to flatter him. However, by seeing what interpretation a lively, fearless girl like Elizabeth puts on his speeches, he is enlightened as to what he 'really' meant—the underlying assumptions and prejudices that, unknown to him until this time, have formed part of his attitude. His character thus develops in response to Elizabeth's own, and this implies, naturally, that he forms a real relationship with her, and the reader therefore can understand why, almost despite himself, he is attracted to her.

All the same one senses that Elizabeth is not fully aware. And this is confirmed a few chapters later when Wickham confides to her the way he has been treated by Darcy:

'I had not thought Mr Darcy so bad as this [she replies]—though I have never liked him, I had not thought so very ill of him—I had supposed him to be despising his fellowcreatures in general, but did not suspect him of descending to such malicious revenge, such injustice, such inhumanity as this!'

After a few minutes' reflection, however, she continued, 'I do remember his boasting one day, at Netherfield, of the implacability of his resentments, of his having an unforgiving temper. His disposition must be dreadful.' (80)

Because Darcy's speech was open to Elizabeth's immediate interpretation, and because her reply to him in the passage quoted above is so quick and lively, there seems at first nothing wrong here. But in the earlier dialogue the phrase 'implacable resentment' is Elizabeth's own, unconsciously now put into Darcy's mouth: she is forgetting that, on the spot, Darcy corrected her. The misremembering is so natural, so native to the character's vivacious ego, that it would obviously be wrong to feel superior to Elizabeth here. At the same time, when you have read the novel more than once, you can detect the slip, and be amused at how much Elizabeth's mind in this conversation is muddled by her obvious attraction to Mr Wickham's masculine charms.

The real 'implacable resentment' in the exchange is Elizabeth's perhaps rather than Darcy's. When Darcy engages Elizabeth for a dance, Charlotte consoles her with 'I dare say you will find him very agreeable', and Elizabeth replies 'Heaven forbid! That would be the greatest misfortune of all! To find a man agreeable whom one is determined to hate!' Like most of Elizabeth's remarks, this one has an exaggeration that reveals it is not meant entirely seriously. But the question of resentment is resumed while Darcy and Elizabeth are dancing, and Elizabeth's comments on being 'blinded by prejudice' also have a reference that she is not aware of. Austen has the ability to make the reader share, sympathize with and participate in life on the same terms as her heroine, whilst at the same time he or she is privileged to understand the mistakes she is making.

Pride and Prejudice, then, is a novel that unites a romantic plot with an argument about contemporary civilisation and society. Elizabeth and Darcy's story is combined with an examination of the precarious position of young unmarried women in the genteel world. The novel refounds the notion of the gentleman, and through this implicitly advocates the new kind of society which is to develop in the nineteenth century. But *Pride and Prejudice* is not located in a precise historical time-frame, unlike the three other great novels discussed in the following chapters.

2

Mansfield Park

Mansfield Park was published in 1814, only a year after *Pride and Prejudice*, but moving from one novel to the other the reader is keenly aware of a change of tone and atmosphere. Partly it is that *Mansfield Park* is evidently the work of an older, maturer, woman. The narrator is not an intrusive presence, by any means, but one who, while an insider of the world she depicts, can also see beyond it. 'Poor woman! she probably thought change of air might agree with many of her children', she remarks of the beleaguered Mrs Price at the conclusion of Chapter 1 (*MP* 11). It is a voice with a range of sympathy beyond the social commonwealth of rich families that is the milieu of *Mansfield Park*.

Almost everyone in this novel is wealthy. Sir Thomas Bertram is a Member of Parliament with a large estate and property in the West Indies; Henry Crawford also has an estate, and enough income easily to afford to have it totally 'improved' as soon as he comes of age. His sister Mary has twenty thousand. Mr Rushworth has a park five miles round and a Tudor mansion. Told that Henry Crawford has 'four thousand a year', Mrs Rushworth senior seems to feel that this is just enough to get by on: 'Very well.—Those who have not more, must be satisfied with what they have' (118). Mr Rushworth in fact is richer even than Darcy. These are all 'young people of fortune', better off than those in any other Austen novel, and untroubled, despite Sir Thomas' need to see to his Antigua estates, by any sense of financial insecurity. Only Mrs Norris is obsessed with saving, a neurotic compensation for her inferior family position whose other manifestation is her remorseless bullying of her even poorer niece, Fanny Price. In part the novel is a study in the assumptions and manners of the very rich, in the manners of 'Society', as the initial conversation between the Crawfords and the Bertrams about 'coming out' (48–51), indicates. Spoilt, full of self-consequence, good looking, healthy, the Bertrams do not need to be proud like Lady Catherine de Bourgh or Sir Walter Elliot. Their vanity is in such good order that they can appear free of it. Lordly, careless, insouciant, and selfish, Tom Bertram at least has some sense of humour.

In *Pride and Prejudice*, the great estate of Pemberley is viewed by a visitor and outsider, and Elizabeth Bennet gives it all the awe and respect of one who can say only that she is 'a gentleman's daughter'. But in *Mansfield Park*, the reader is, so to speak, a resident, shown what it is like to live from day to day in such a place. The spaciousness of the house is an important factor in the lives and events that the novel traces, and much of Austen's narrational skill in the brilliant first volume consists in the manipulation and interweaving of a large number of characters and destinies within one locale that is also a group of distinct spaces. For Fanny, the novel's uprooted heroine, '[t]he grandeur of the house astonished, but could not console her. The rooms were too large for her to move in with ease. Whatever she touched she expected to injure, and she crept about in constant terror of something or other' (14–15). Just taken away from her mother and her family, Fanny projects onto the furniture her own sense of the potential injuriousness of this space, felt to be both empty and hostile. Mansfield is not, on the whole, a glamorous or idyllic home (until it becomes such in Fanny's eyes at the end of the novel). Harassed and disregarded, Fanny gradually constructs a surrogate maternal space to which to withdraw and find consolation; furnishing the East room with discarded bric-a-brac and carelessly donated gifts, she makes a fragile 'nest of comforts' that is an emotional as well as physical improvisation. But this room which Fanny thinks of as 'her own', that she has made her own, is always actually marked as the room of a dependent, a transient, by the absence of a fire in the grate.

Jane Austen's ability to make the setting integral to her development of character can be illustrated too, by the early scene where the youthful Fanny is waiting for Mary Crawford to return with the mare that she has borrowed. She is scolded out of the house by Mrs Norris and discerns the party of Edmund, Mary, and the groomsmen in the distance across the park. 'The sound of merriment ascended even to her' (67): the phrasing subtly makes Fanny's geographical separation from the group a simultaneous index of her emotional isolation. 'After a few minutes, they stopt entirely, Edmund was close to her, he was speaking to her, he was evidently directing her management of the bridle, he had hold of her hand; she saw it, or the imagination supplied what the eye could not reach' (67). The careful punctuation of the passage supplies a tempo to the rhythm that communicates the undercurrent of Fanny's jealousy. She 'sees', her imagination inflamed by her feelings, more than her eye actually 'reaches'. After this passage, the attentive reader can be in no doubt that Fanny's love for Edmund is a sexual, not a sibling passion.

From one point of view, Fanny Price is an interesting psychological study in the manners and attitudes of a radically insecure and even traumatized personality. The impatience that one inevitably feels with some of her more censorious or prim judgments, and her more stilted efforts at conversation, may be moderated by the careful history of displacement Austen has provided for her, her years of unremitting intimidation by Mrs Norris, and her youthful dependence on an Edmund whose kindnesses come along with a good deal of tutorly instruction. Her disapproving attitude towards Mary is always complicated by its jealous colouring as well as an even more disqualifying trait, envy. Fanny's moral attitudes in general are overdetermined—part the result of Edmund's coaching, part the result of her own nature and insecurities—and so it is a great simplification to see her as modelling a 'conduct book', a Christian, or an Evangelical heroine. If she is 'prim' or a 'prig' as some critics have called her, that, the novel shows, is a consequence of her situation: an intensely intelligent girl condemned to spend her days sorting out Lady Bertram's knitting, she has constructed an inner world for herself from her reading. It is better to think of her as mildly autistic, rather than a prig, in the sense that her inner life, constructed analogously to the 'nest of comforts', is derived from her private study of literature. Her stilted, over-intellectual attempts to contribute to conversations, which may make modern readers impatient, are Austen's representation of a person whose intense inner world is not reciprocated in the outer circumstances of her life. No-one quite simply, besides Edmund, has thought her worth talking to. As Fanny's quotations of Scott, in particular, disclose, her imaginative inner world is filled with 'enthusiasm' or romantic longing.

Mansfield Park is a novel in the mode of the omniscient narrator, and for the first and only time, Jane Austen continuously allows the narrative to move freely in and out of the consciousnesses of a whole range of characters. In *Pride and Prejudice*, there are moments, especially early in the novel, when Darcy's and Charlotte Lucas' thoughts are presented. In *Persuasion*, the reader is shown at one crucial moment Captain Wentworth's still-burning anger against Anne. But in *Mansfield Park* the independence of the narrator from any one controlling consciousness is a structural principle. This text at various times represents the thinking processes or picks up the internal speech-cadences of Maria Bertram, Edmund Bertram, Sir Thomas, Mary Crawford, and several others, besides Fanny Price. When Sir Thomas overhears Mr Yates in full ranting flight on the improvised stage at Mansfield the narrative borrows his point of view at the beginning of the paragraph, and, to heighten the comic effect, Tom Bertram's at the close (182–3).

Perhaps most significantly, this novel presents whole scenes and dialogues from which the heroine is absent. The dialogues at the Parsonage between Mary and Henry Crawford (and sometimes with Mrs Grant) are quite freestanding. They depict the relationship between the Crawfords at first without reference to Fanny. Thus the novel is structured with two different centres or foci of interest. In the mode of 'free indirect speech', Mary's thoughts about her prospects on entering a new place and about older brothers, for example, are allowed to enter the text without authorial commentary. Following from these gay and brilliant introductory scenes (Volume I, Chapters 4 and 5) the narrator naturally keeps the reader in touch with Mary Crawford's private thoughts—she has been given the representational treatment of a major figure, and her projects accordingly draw some sympathetic attention. It is not just the fact that Mary is vivacious, while the supposed heroine Fanny is timid and nervous, that makes for this novel's moral complications: it is that the rival figures are each accorded an almost equivalent narrative stature until Fanny's removal to Portsmouth in the last volume.

The reporting of Mary's thoughts moves fluidly between the medium of indirect speech, the dramatic representation of her behaviour, and direct commentary on both. But if *Mansfield Park* is a more 'difficult' text than the other Austen novels, it is because different modes, or rather dimensions or aspects, of presentation throughout the novel tend to suggest different judgments or agendas. For example, when Sir Thomas Bertram interviews Maria and asks her whether she wants to press on with the engagement to Rushworth (200–1) his thoughts are outlined like an internal monologue without quotation marks. The reader is expected to see through the self-deceptions and convenient blindnesses of his reasonings, but to retain the vestigial sympathy one conventionally has for a figure whose thought-processes, whose capacity to reflect, one has intimately followed. The caustic comments that follow—'Such and such-like were the reasonings of Sir Thomas . . .'—are an abrupt shift of address, and require a change of attitude from the reader from participatory leniency to dismissive contempt. These differing narrative approaches (not always as abrupt as here) are one source of the novel's scintillating life, but they sometimes cause ethical tension in the reader that is not entirely resolved.

The presentation of Mary and Henry Crawford, freestanding, but doubled through the perspective of the heroine, is the major instance of this challenge. Mary has lived in London and has a range of social skills that are apparently worldly and sophisticated, but viewed from Fanny's position, she often seems sadly tactless. One complication of her tone—her 'sweet peculiarity of manner' as Edmund fondly describes it—is a tincture of disillusionment that is not quite as cynical as she imagines. The sketch of Mary's years at the Admiral's house that emerges from her allusions, however witty and professedly unconcerned, indicates a history that invites sympathy for a damaged life. When she is married, she tells Mrs Grant, she will be a staunch defender of the marriage state, and adds 'I wish my friends in general would be so too. It would save me many a heart-ache' (47). Her disrespectful description of her uncle's household—'of *Rears* and *Vices*, I saw enough'—is witty, but the self-conscious daring of the wit is defensive: it laughs off a miserable past that bears heavily upon her. 'In short, it is not a favourite profession of mine. It has never worn an amiable form to *me*' (60). The remarks scandalize Fanny and Edmund, but their intensity, which is replicated whenever Mary brings up the topic of life at the Admiral's, betrays an experience that is clearly formative. Mary's unhappy family history, brought up in the charge of her aunt and uncle, mirrors Fanny's, and a reader might justly suppose that the traumatic effects of her adoptive home on one personality are as relevant to the author's purpose as they are on the other. In other words, though Mary's worldliness is viewed critically (through the eyes of Fanny and Edmund especially) it is also readable as a coping strategy, a sign of an insecurity much less manifest than Fanny's, but a key part of the personality.

The complications of feeling and judgment these different dimensions of narration give rise to can be exemplified by the memorable scene when Mrs Norris turns on Fanny and accuses her of being 'a very obstinate, ungrateful girl . . . very ungrateful indeed, considering who and what she is' (147). The setting is the drawing room, where Tom, Maria, Henry Crawford, and Mr Yates are at a table with the play in front of them, while Lady Bertram on her sofa, Edmund, Fanny, and Mrs Norris are grouped nearer the fire. The separation is political. Mary Crawford's predicament and nervousness (she wants Edmund to act the Anhalt role but does not know how to approach the issue) is defined by her movement between one and the other set of people within the room. She shifts from group to group, in response to different promptings, her freedom a sign not of independence but of her need to attach herself, to find a centre for her emotional life, almost, one might say, to find a home. When Edmund snubs her, she 'was silenced; and with some feelings of resentment and mortification', the reader is told, 'moved her chair' towards Mrs Norris at the tea-table.

The reader's main focus is on Fanny, who is the target of Tom's plans, so that the little drama of Mary's manoeuvres interweaves it only as a subsidiary theme. The climax is Tom's repeated 'attack' on Fanny and Mrs Norris' angry speech. Mary's immediate response is 'I do not like my situation; this *place* is too hot for me' and her moving of her chair once again to the opposite side of the table. Mary's action, the completion of her series of movements, is sympathetically described as she continues to talk to Fanny and to try 'to raise her spirits, in spite of being out of spirits herself'. But in a moment one's admiration for her courage and kindness becomes undermined: 'By a look to her brother, she prevented any farther entreaty from the theatrical board, and the really good feelings by which she was almost purely governed, were rapidly restoring her to all the little she had lost in Edmund's favour' (147). This odd sentence, beginning with Mary's (or the narrator's) point of view and ending with Edmund's, seems to attribute to him an unwarranted insight into Mary's motives, and the upshot is a carping note all-too-consonant with the suspiciousness of Fanny. The dramas of the two young women have been presented contrapuntally, but at this point where their projects actually clash, the task of keeping sympathy for both figures alive in the narrative proves just too much. This episode presents a miniature version of the narrative knot that Austen cuts in the last section of the novel by removing Fanny to Portsmouth and allowing only her consciousness to preside.

'By a look to her brother': the reader's responses to Mary Crawford are also complicated by the fact that the dialogues between Mary and Henry bring out their mutual rapport. They seem to have a family style, teasing, humorous, generous, that contrasts with the absence of anything like wit or style among the Bertrams. One never sees Julia and Maria, who are said to get on well, for example, in conversation, and Tom only speaks to Edmund in order to make clear who is boss. Henry, as Mary declares, 'loves me, consults me, confides in me' (59). Henry's regard for Mary invites the reader to see his flirtations with Maria and Julia in a light that is perhaps a shade different from the youthful Fanny's abhorrence. (Mary's resolve to keep her affections under control also cannot but make one despise Maria's sulky disregard of consequences.) Thus the Crawfords' worldliness is accompanied by a complicating un-Bertramesque mutuality, kindness, and adult consideration. The narrator celebrates the 'fraternal' tie (235) explicitly in reference to Fanny and William Price, but only with the Crawfords does the novel dramatise it vividly.

Henry Crawford is as marked as his sister by the arrangements in his uncle's household. Fatherless and allowed a free rein by the Admiral, Henry does not require the approval of others to feel justified in what he does: in fact he rather relishes opposition than the reverse, which perhaps explains his persistence in the courtship of the anything but graciously reluctant Fanny. Henry's pursuit of his sexual objects, in this instance Maria, is accompanied by contempt for those objects. Austen implies that he has picked up such attitudes from his uncle. But she also succeeds in suggesting how his spoilt and liberal upbringing can result in fascination when the beloved offers the challenge, but also the comfort, of inflexible resistance. "'I could so wholly and absolutely confide in her," said he; "and that is what I want"' (294).

Henry's courtship of Fanny is accompanied by conversations in which he discusses it with Mary, and his love for Fanny by her endorsement, or perhaps, collusion. The dual focus is most brilliantly exploited in Chapters 11 and 12 of the second volume. For many chapters, the novel has seen events mainly from the standpoint of Fanny Price. It is her view of Henry's flirtations that has been given, her mistrust, resentment, and reluctance have been highlighted, even while it is counterpointed and ironically at odds with the excitements and delights of the Crawfords. After the ball, which Sir Thomas has organized from the barely conscious wish to promote Fanny's chances with Henry, Edmund goes away to be ordained. In Chapter 11, Fanny's state of mind is described, but then the narrative shifts its focus on to Mary at the Parsonage. It is now she whose thoughts are filled with anxiety and self-mistrust, and who now contends 'with one disagreeable emotion entirely new to her—jealousy' (286). The positions of the two young women have been reversed as Mary tries to extract some reassurance of her power over Edmund from the unbending Miss Price.

In Volume II, Chapter 12, Henry returns and announces, to Mary's astonishment, that he intends to marry Fanny Price. The genius of this almost entirely dramatic scene is that it gives full recognition to the excitement, gaiety and exhilaration of the two figures who challenge the narrative and moral status of the hero and heroine. The reader's responses are not inhibited by reservations from the narrator. What also makes it so telling is that it is not merely a scene of mutual delight and congratulation, but that it touches once more on the painful family history that has made these two, and their needs, what they are. Henry, even while he acknowledges the grossness of his uncle, says of him, 'Few fathers would have let me half so much.' In the midst of her delight, with her mind racing ahead to what this means for her own prospects, Mary stops and sounds a sombre note: 'Henry, I think so highly of Fanny Price, that if I could suppose the next Mrs Crawford would have half the reason which my poor ill used aunt had to abhor the very name, I would prevent the marriage, if possible' (296). This is Mary's best moment in the novel: she speaks from the depths of her experience and with moral authority. Her unhappy background leads her, in this very exchange, to fantasize a reconstituted family—cousins and brother and sister—together in Northamptonshire, a fantasy that ironically duplicates some of Fanny's own longings.

It is not only its psychological depth and its narrative orchestration that make *Mansfield Park* a milestone in the English novel. The novelist imagines the physical world in which her figures move to have a palpable presence, an effective bearing on their lives. At one point in *Pride and Prejudice*, the narrator remarks casually on 'the shrubbery where this conversation took place' (*P&P* 86). Settings are never neutral in *Mansfield Park*, and the gardens at Sotherton, famously, are made to play an integral, even determinative part in the action. It is not only that one can read them in allegorical terms, as the punning exchange of Henry and Maria about her 'prospects' naturally invites. It is rather as if emotional pressures and urgencies were felt, and conveyed to the reader, in spatial terms, as when Maria declares so intensely 'I cannot get out, as the starling said' (*MP* 99). As the figures move, disperse and reassemble within the various venues Sotherton and Mansfield and Portsmouth provide, the reader is made vividly aware not only of the opportunities and inhibitions of these spaces, but of their being at issue— contested over, claimed and owned. Maria's disregard of the locked gate is to be echoed in Tom's overturning the arrangements of his father's rooms: both express their selfish drives as the usurpation of territory. Fanny seeks to keep Edmund at the window looking at the stars, Mary lures him indoors with her music. Characters and their embodiment are imagined precisely within settings that are drawn into the narrative and act as provocations to conversation and action.

This capacity to dramatize space and to make the human drama inseparable from its physical location reaches its peak in the scenes at Portsmouth. As Edward Said observes, for example, the 'solitary candle' that Fanny's father holds 'between himself and the paper, without any reference to her possible convenience' (382) 'renders very precisely the dangers of unsociability, of lonely insularity, of diminished awareness that are rectified in larger and better administered spaces'. It is this evening that Fanny remembers three months later when her depression is deepened by the sun that brings its glare to illuminate the dirt and disorder of her parents' parlour. When she returns to Mansfield with Edmund in early spring, an affiliation between emotional state, narrative purpose, and landscape setting—the trees in 'that delightful state . . . while much is actually given to the sight, more yet remains for the imagination' (446–7)—suggests the possibilities that are to be explored further in *Emma* and *Persuasion*.

3

Emma

The social setting and conceptual structure of *Emma* are quite
different from *Mansfield Park*. From the vigorously trochaic
rhythm of the opening words—'Emma Woodhouse, handsome,
clever and rich . . .'—a confident, energetic, and commanding
voice carries this narrative forwards. This is an optimistic book,
coloured by Emma's 'eager laughing warmth', very much
conceived of as a comedy, with the cross-purposes,
misunderstandings, mistaken identities, tricking, and teasing
that are definitive of comedy as a genre. In the vicinity of
Emma, the narrative picks up her tone, her expressions, her
phrasing, even when it is not formally committed to rendering
her speech or thought-patterns. Occasionally, there is a note
that does not belong to her, as in the description of
Mrs Weston's thoughts on her marriage: 'She felt herself a
most fortunate woman; and she had lived long enough to
know how fortunate she might well be thought, where the
only regret was for a partial separation from friends, whose
friendship for her had never cooled, and who could ill bear to
part with her!' (*E* 18). This is the voice of an older, sadder
woman than Emma, which might not be out of place in
Mansfield Park or *Persuasion*.

But for the most part the narrative voice of *Emma*, while
flexible, and capable even of picking up Mr Elton's vulgarisms
when in his vicinity, is overwhelmingly the style of Emma

Woodhouse, youthful, confident, presumptive, witty, dogmatic, commanding, assured. 'Harriet was to sit again the next day; and Mr Elton, just as he ought, entreated for the permission of attending and reading to them again' (47). Though this is formally information given by the narrator, the phrase 'just as he ought' construes his motives according to Emma's point of view. Sometimes one can catch the narrator assuming Emma's viewpoint deliberately to trick the reader. A few moments later Mrs Weston is said to talk to Mr Elton of Miss Smith 'not in the least suspecting she was addressing a lover'; Frank Churchill, pressed to visit the Bates', is said to consent only 'with the hope of Hartfield to reward him' (235). In each of these cases, Emma's view of motives is allowed to tease the reader, to appear as if it is the book's.

So everything—more or less—is shown through Emma Woodhouse's eyes. Charged with her own spirits and energy and self-consequence, she shapes the narrated world according to her presumptions, pre-conceptions, and demands. The structural principle of the novel, this is formally broken with only twice. The scene in Volume I, Chapter 5 in which Mr Knightley and Mrs Weston discuss Emma in her absence, is matched by Chapter 5 in Volume III, in which Mr Knightley's suspicions of a liaison between Jane Fairfax and Frank Churchill seem to be confirmed by their behaviour over the word game. As Mr Knightley watches them in the gathering darkness of the room, he questions his observations—as Emma never does. Later a looser style of narrative takes over, but in the first two volumes the tunnelling of vision produces some of its most amusing and delicious effects.

But if the novel is bounded by this rule (a flexible rule) it is also bounded spatially. *Emma* is a narrative in which circumscribed settings, limited spaces, and confinement (comforting and enabling, but at the same time imprisoning and suffocating) are crucially important. Highbury, the country village almost the size of a town, in which the novel is set, is conceptually, if not geographically, isolated from the rest of the world. Augusta Elton lets it be known that Mr Elton has expressed fears 'lest the retirement' of Highbury be dis-agreeable to his bride (276), and recommending Bath to

Emma, comments that 'it would be a charming introduction for you, who have lived so secluded a life'. She also thinks that Jane Fairfax is wasting her sweetness on the desert air. Highbury is provincial and confined—a citystate, a commonwealth, that Frank Churchill takes out his freedom in by purchasing gloves at Ford's and declaring *his amor patriae* (200). (The true freedom of Highbury, of course, is won by the hard work of parish meetings and neighbourly concern that Mr Knightley puts in.)

Yet to speak of Highbury's isolation and limitedness is to put the emphasis mistakenly. 'Our lot is cast in a goodly heritage', effuses Miss Bates, and Highbury is depicted as a cheerfully functioning community (it is 'reckoned a particularly healthy spot'). For despite Emma's wariness—her wish not quite to define her identity in terms of the place—Highbury is not seen from the position of an amused or superior outside observer (as 'Cranford' is seen in Elizabeth Gaskell's later Victorian novel). Though the reader sees from one point of view, and that one rather given to snobbery, the novel generates, especially in Volume II, a sense of busy interplay between characters and between social classes, a network of visiting, gossip, charitable acts, and neighbourly concern.

One of the achievements of the novel is to populate 'the Highbury world' (352) and give it apparent depth. The loose ends and superfluous names that figure so much in Miss Bates' gossip do not just serve to camouflage the essential bits of information that she is feeding into the plot, they are a technically adroit means of conveying, especially in the Highbury ball scene, this sense of a social commonwealth. It is not only in Miss Bates' speeches that characters are spoken of familiarly who are never formally presented. Mr Perry, the doctor who may or may not be setting up his carriage, is only the most frequently mentioned of a host of figures who pass in and out of the narrative and acquire a kind of familiarity by proxy. It is as if by having William Larkins, Robert Martin, Mrs Goddard, and many others—Mrs Hodges, John Abdy, Patty, James, the Coxes, even the Coles—partially within our field of vision, the novel persuades us of their richly extended existence beyond it.

The novelist makes sure that the reader grasps that the

curtailment of space—this drawing of strict boundaries—has social and ethical dimensions too. She introduces a scene in which Emma and Harriet visit a poor cottage (Volume I, Chapter 10). The walk on the way offers opportunity for some of Emma's more preposterous pronouncements about herself but it also serves to define the parameters of the novel's scheme. This is a part of Highbury that is not part of Emma's Highbury, and Emma's words on surveying the cottage define the limitations of the conceptual world of the novel (not to be confused with the historical social world of Regency England). Emma and Harriet cross 'the low hedge, and tottering footstep which ended the narrow, slippery path through the cottage garden, and brought them into the lane again'. Emma tells Harriet that her impression of the misery in the cottage will not soon be over. '"I do not think it will"', she says, 'stopping to look once more at all the outward wretchedness of the place, and recall the still greater within' (87). Then, 'the lane made a slight bend; and when that bend was passed, Mr Elton was immediately in sight' and the novel resumes its comic intrigue: an elegant way for the novelist to put out of sight, out of the novel's focus, a whole aspect of Highbury life. The episode is relevant to the novel's concern with charity in all its forms, but what it also does is persuade the reader to see how geographical space, moral focus, and conceptual scheme can be identified.

Emma and Harriet's walk is an interruption to the sequence of Hartfield scenes in the first volume of the novel. Women in *Emma* are more or less limited to drawing rooms, but men can walk in at all hours, and even go off to London for a haircut. Jane Fairfax is subject to a neighbourly inquisition when she is caught walking in the rain to the local post office on the chance of hearing from her beloved, but Mr Knightley is free to ride through the rain all the way from London to attend to the needs of his. Space is thus gendered, and the various dimensions of confinement interrelated: confinement to the indoors, to a restricted sphere of influence, to a small community; and on the other hand, freedom to enjoy the outdoors, freedom to exercise choice, to travel. The reader is asked to see a correlation, or correspondence, between being shut in and the possibilities of the moral life, as when Emma, pronouncing with ineffable complacency to Harriet that she will never get married, says 'those who live perforce in a very small, and generally very inferior, society, may well be illiberal and cross' (85).

In *Emma* women's imprisonment is associated with deprivation, with energies and powers perverted in their application, and events, balls, and outings are linked with the arousal and satisfaction of desire. But the presentation is not black and white: structure is perceived to be essential to the fulfilment of desire, and the freedom of the outdoors is depicted as potentially treacherous or empty. The novel's own momentum harnesses Emma's and the reader's desire for expansion and the release of energies. Confined to Hartfield for most of the first volume, the narrative then gradually expands its horizons with an increasingly far-flung series of outings, visits, and the ball at the Crown, until it climaxes in the two excursions, one a day after the other, a chapter after the other, to Donwell and to Box Hill. Then, when Emma learns of Harriet's great expectations of Mr Knightley, there is a scene set in her father's drawing room in which the term 'prospect' (422), as in *Mansfield Park*, requires us to read the confined room, the miserable weather outside included, as both the material condition of Emma's melancholy, and a metaphor.

But Emma, like other ladies, does make visits. One particularly skilful exploitation of her point of view is the passage (literally) between Chapter 9 and Chapter 10 of Volume II in which the reader, accompanying Emma and pursued 'by the sounds of [Miss Bates'] desultory good will' climbs the stairs to the Bates' apartment and (over the page, opening the next chapter) sees the room as if the curtain has gone up on a stage set. 'The appearance of the little sitting-room as they entered, was tranquillity itself; Mrs Bates, deprived of her usual employment, slumbering on one side of the fire, Frank Churchill, at a table near her, most deedily occupied about her spectacles, and Jane Fairfax, standing with her back to them, intent on her pianoforte' (240). This is what Emma sees, and the following sequence in which Frank encourages her suspicions of Jane while at the same time speaking otherwise to his fiancée is a particularly delicious example of his skill, or damning evidence of his duplicity (depending on how one's sympathies lie). While we read the following scene from Emma's point of view, and are involved in Emma's responses—among them that characteristic shading of her hostility to Jane into pity and back again—the novelist is inviting the reader to step beyond her and to see it quite differently. That 'deedily occupied' raises the suspicion that the young occupants have just sprung into these innocent positions. Poor old Mrs Bates has been as effectually blinded as Emma.

Because of the confinement of focus to Emma, Frank Churchill is presented entirely dramatically and therefore enigmatically: is he appeasing or teasing Emma when he professes to take up all her suspicions regarding Jane Fairfax? How much is he being ironic at her expense when he says 'but I, simple I, saw nothing but the fact . . . I do not mean to say, however, that you might not have made discoveries' (218)? When he murmurs about 'conjecture'—'aye, sometimes one conjectures right and sometimes one conjectures wrong'— what kind of adroit act is he performing? In retrospect, one might be sure that he's slyly implying the same criticisms of Emma that Mr Knightley makes so forthrightly, but the reader, listening with Emma's ears, laps up the flattery that his words appear to proffer. Frank is not merely a manipulator: Austen's presentation allows one to detect his moments of bad conscience, of uneasiness at the game he is forced into, as well as his enjoyment of the game itself—'Then I will speak the truth, and nothing suits me so well' (200). The reader is free to imagine that Frank is both sly and impetuous—that he is always straining against the restrictions of secrecy and at the same time enjoying the opportunities for mischief it presents. The enigmatic and mercurial nature of the character is a product of the technique of presentation adopted. For reasons best known to himself, Mr Knightley does not think much of him.

Neither does Mr Woodhouse. 'That young man is not quite the thing' (or: 'not what he ought to be'). Frank dares to break the Highbury habit of deference to Mr Perry, and, even more scandalously, provokes Mr Woodhouse into panic over open windows at the ball. 'Open the windows! . . . Nobody could be so imprudent! I never heard of such a thing. Dancing with open windows! I am sure neither your father nor Mrs Weston (poor Miss Taylor that was) would suffer it.' And Frank replies, 'Ah! sir—but a thoughtless young person will sometimes step behind a window-curtain, and throw up a sash without its being suspected. I have often known it done myself' (251–2). The reader may well enjoy this teasing, as with Mr John Knightley's earlier and much less good-tempered taunts about the snow thick on the ground at Randalls.

Frank throws open windows in the novel in a more modern sense—the opportunity of viewing the characters and events within a different ethic. If we laugh with him, we enjoy a temporary truancy from the official morality of the novel's conceptual world. Frank presents the possibility of seeing things another way—one that allows much more to impetuosity and surprise, to passion and risk-taking. In this view Mr Woodhouse would be seen as blocking the way, a man whose depressive fussiness inhibits and shuts down opportunities and possibilities of life, and Mr Knightley's masculine rationality and rule-giving an attempt to contain and organize a world that is actually much more volatile. Yet since Emma's perspective is so much the novel's, the reader who takes out his or her freedom in Highbury undertakes to accept its consensus and thus declines to pursue these options or doubts.

Emma, of course, is completely unaware of the relationship between Frank and Jane. But her misunderstanding is deeper than this. What she misses in Frank and Jane's situation is a romantic element that is deeply foreign to her temperament. For Emma the arrival of the piano is simply a stimulus for further speculation about Mr Dixon: the gift might have been a piece of jewellery (an amber cross?) for all the difference it makes. But the choice of the piano as a gift is not accidental. It becomes clear that Jane and Frank fell in love over music, and that music is important to Jane in a way that Emma cannot fully conceive. In this very scene Frank manages to say to Jane, '"I believe you were glad we danced no longer; but I would have given worlds—all the worlds one ever has to give—

for another half hour." She played' (242). Jane speaks, in effect, through the piano. Her eloquence passes unheard by Emma. Later, preoccupied by thoughts about Mr Knightley, she scarcely notices 'the sweet sounds of the united voices' of Frank and Jane singing in the background. Only through music does the community unwittingly sanction their intimacy. One is left to speculate that perhaps it is an insight into her confined circumstances and the need for an outlet that has motivated the gift of the piano, a gift 'thoroughly from the heart', attuned to the needs of the beloved, as Frank contrives to declare. Moreover, a piano is a symbol of culture and gentility—as the discussion at Mrs Cole's brings out—and the present is a pledge on Frank's part of a future larger, more comprehensive in its cultural horizons, than the Bates' two rooms. When the engagement is broken off, and Jane faces a future as governess, Miss Bates reports her addressing the piano directly: 'Poor dear Jane was talking of it just now. "You must go", said she. "You and I must part. You will have no business here"' (384).

Frank's gift of the piano is therefore loaded with implications—cultural, social, and erotic—that Emma cannot see. But mostly it is that the piano signifies passion. So that while Emma is busily constructing a tawdry romantic narrative around Jane, and taking Frank to be confirming her speculations, the reader is at the same time being given the material to substantiate a conception of love that is, indeed, romantic—a love that seems to have been more or less at first sight, that is expressed by both in passionate terms, and that is carried on in defiance of social proprieties. 'Had she refused', to become engaged, Frank later writes, 'I should have gone mad' (437). This intensity—Jane herself, not given to gush, speaks of Frank's 'bewitching' qualities—is all the more remarkable because it conflicts with, or is set up in opposition to, the notion of companionate love that is developed through the novel's focus on *Emma*. For Emma, which celebrates rational marriage, also offers credence to passionate and reckless love.

Austen's interweaving of the suggestions of a deeply romantic narrative within the novel is the more telling because its main 'love story' is such a fundamental revision of the convention. Though superficially the relationship of Emma

Woodhouse and Mr Knightley resembles the pupil/tutor pattern that is discernible in Catherine Morland and Henry Tilney, Fanny and Edmund, and even Elizabeth and Darcy—he is so much older than she, for example—it is far more than these a relationship of equals, even though Emma is a woman and thus severely restricted in the ways she can exercise power, and in the forms her intelligence can take. Theirs are contests between equals in confidence, wit, and capacity for strong and sympathetic feeling. Both love everything that is decided and open. When they fight over Harriet Smith and Robert Martin, Emma may 'abuse her reason' but it is as if, underlying the real anger and indignation on both sides, there is a reciprocation of energy, a love of the other's strength of mind. The real identity of Emma and Knightley's views is defined in their next quarrel when Emma 'to her great amusement, perceived that she was taking the other side of the question from her real opinion' (145): the underlying and unconscious motive is clearly pleasure in crossing swords with Mr Knightley.

Emma finds Mr Knightley such a stimulus to her ingenuity that the reader may well feel swayed by her arguments. 'You are very fond of bending little minds; but when little minds belong to rich people in authority, I think they have a knack of swelling out, till they are quite as unmaneageable as great ones' (147). Like so much of what Emma says, this has the ring of intuitive truth. Some readers think that Mr Knightley is never wrong, and, in the sense that the outcomes of Emma's meddling with Harriet's life are much as he predicts, they are correct: but dramatically, Emma's ideas—just because they capture something of a world that is less tractable, more random and ungovernable than Mr Knightley's own good sense and rationality allow—have a good deal of value, and what the reader watches, as a spectacle, is Emma's wit and fire in Mr Knightley's presence. And in a later dispute, when Mr Knightley says that Mrs Elton would be subdued by Miss Fairfax into deference, and Emma doubts it, her more open sense of unpredictability and volatility in human relations certainly scores over him.

This is a relation in which, then, the erotic content is always implicit, always transmuted or sublimated. Mr Knightley only learns how he feels about Emma from his own jealousy of Frank. Emma's desire for Mr Knightley (as distinct from her admiration and regard for him) is out of her own awareness— impeded by her devotion to her father. So the novel needs to find ways to convey to the reader that the marriage with which it will inevitably close is plausible, has to make the reader desire Emma's union with Mr Knightley, has to find ways of conveying her unconscious erotic or desiring attachment to him. 'She always declares she will never marry, which, of course, means just nothing at all' (41), Mr Knightley has said: Emma declares as much to Harriet, and a good deal of the comedy of the novel concerns, of course, Emma's own pursuit of romantic matters by proxy. Austen shows, too, that Knightley is constantly in Emma's thoughts, but cumulatively these, and even the telling moment at the ball when she registers his 'tall, firm, upright figure' (336), do not quite amount convincingly to a demonstration of hidden desire. But perhaps the most effective technique for persuading the reader of the necessity of the marriage is the interlude of description of Donwell Abbey.

In this, as in so much else, *Emma* is a rewriting of *Pride and Prejudice*. The crucial point in the evolution of Elizabeth's feelings towards Mr Darcy is her visit to Pemberley, where she sees him at home, at ease in his own setting, and given a glowing personal reference by his own housekeeper. It is evident that Pemberley, the estate, has a metonymic relation to its owner: it not only symbolizes or represents his social and financial status, but gives material presence to less definable qualities like his taste and his judgment. Even more than this: the stream abounds with fish, and the table, when Elizabeth visits Miss Darcy, is piled with 'beautiful pyramids of grapes, nectarines and peaches' (*P&P* 268).

Donwell Abbey is introduced into the narrative at about the same point, and is a set-piece of a similar kind. Both houses represent, or figure forth, their owners. Pemberley is manifestly an image of social power and wealth. Donwell Abbey is more complex; less idealized, less in the image of houses and their grounds 'improved' by Repton or Capability Brown. 'It was just what it ought to be, and it looked what it was'

(*E* 358). Donwell Abbey, as Emma views it, has its limitations—
the disputable taste of the walk, its neglect of prospect—it is
without fashionable smoothness and thus presents or incarnates
the blunt honesty, the moral integrity, even what Austen
presents as the characteristic Englishness, of its owner. 'Eager
to refresh and correct her memory with more particular
observation, more exact understanding' Emma seizes the
chance to explore alone (her father being temporarily taken
care of) and look about her. She warms to 'its suitable,
becoming, characteristic situation, low and sheltered—its ample
gardens stretching down to meadows washed by a stream . . .
its abundance of timber in rows and avenues' (357–8). Emma
feels a sense of propriety, of possession and affiliation. This is
a spectacle of plenitude and comfort, richness, prosperity, and
containment. Viewing it—and Emma slips off once again 'for
a few moments' free observation of the entrance and ground-
plot of the house' (362)—gives her peculiar relish.

One difference between Donwell and Pemberley is that
Elizabeth Bennet is perfectly conscious that in seeing over it
she is revising her view of Darcy. Emma is unconscious of the
fact that the place is identified for her with its proprietor, that
in being there—indeed in luxuriating in it—she is
unconsciously imagining union with Mr Knightley. She never
thinks: 'To be mistress of Donwell might be something!' Yet
the warmth of her response (here indistinguishable from the
narrator's) is important for moving the narrative impetus
forward. It suggests that Donwell is a place that, while realistic
on the surface (the planning of its gardens is almost as awkward
as Sotherton in *Mansfield Park*) offers a receptacle for dreams.
The house and its surroundings—the farm, the orchard, even
the abundance of strawberries—augur satisfaction, fulfilment,
amplitude. Seeing Harriet and Mr Knightley admiring the
view of the farm, Emma's description warms to 'all its
appendages of prosperity and beauty, its rich pastures,
spreading flocks, orchard in blossom, and light column of
smoke ascending' (360).

In his notes to *Emma*, R.W. Chapman points out that 'the
orchard in blossom' when the season is said to be 'about

Midsummer' is 'one of Miss Austen's very rare mistakes of this kind' (493). The 'light column of smoke ascending' is also oddly unseasonal. But perhaps 'mistake' is too simple an explanation for these effects: what is being presented here is not a place but an idyll, the fantasy of the pastoral paradise. There is an enthusiasm that seeks to represent Donwell and its estate, not just as admirable and august, but as having everything—strawberries at their peak of ripeness, sunshine, 'spreading flocks', 'ample gardens washed by a stream', prosperous farmland, and the domestic hearth: a rich constatation of all that desire encompasses. But by representing Emma's desire in the image of, as contained by, the house, garden, and estate, Jane Austen performs a narrative and ideological hat-trick. Erotic longing is united with a conservative political and social agenda. Emma's desire is not to possess the house, but rather the house is made an eloquent embodiment or vessel for that desire, which is thenceforth seen to be inseparable from the social institutions that may contain it. It is Donwell, thus, that persuades the reader that Emma's destiny is to be with Mr Knightley—persuades one both of the social propriety (in the largest sense of fitness and likelihood of happiness) of the union, but also, more subtly, that Mr Knightley will answer to Emma's needs just as much as to her desires: permanence, strength, and that stability that is also 'abundance', and growth which is an implicit warranty of sexual amplitude.

All this can be accomplished because Donwell is 'low and sheltered': this is an outdoor scene in which freedom is liberty, structured within an ordered, established, social world. At Box Hill, in the next chapter, the open air is an empty space, people wander off in all directions, social relations are unstructured, the limitations of innovation and the tensions of leisure are manifest. Soon follows the scene where Emma, confined to the Hartfield drawing room and with nothing to look forward to but a string of similar evenings with her father, revisits the past: an indoors that encapsulates boredom, frustration and deprivation. When, next day, the proposal takes place, it is in the garden. Here, in this wonderful scene, two intelligent people, each fearing that the other is devoted to another person, try their best to hold back their own emotions, and to give all their energy, their attention, their care, to further the other's happiness.

What Emma learns in this novel is not to think like Mr Knightley, but that she has always, in fact, thought like him. There is no element of capitulation in the novel's ending, rather one of celebratory recognition. Their reconciliation would be the conclusion of a conventional romantic narrative, but Emma and Mr Knightley converse a good deal after their private engagement. Unlike Elizabeth and Darcy who, in a similar situation, educate each other into the intimacy of equals, Emma and Mr Knightley enjoy already their reciprocal knowledge. They chafe and tease each other, working through the past, replaying their relationship in different terms: it is almost as if Austen were presenting Emma and Mr Knightley as an already married couple. These scenes are by no means simply occasions for Emma to confess to being 'wrong'. 'What had she to wish for? Nothing, but to grow more worthy of him, whose intentions and judgment had been ever so superior to her own. Nothing, but that the lessons of her past folly might teach her humility and circumspection in future' (475). This is Emma thinking—vivaciously, but also extravagantly—as usual.

4

Persuasion

Emma Woodhouse occupies her world so vividly that its sparseness—that there has been no ball at the Crown for many years—is hardly noticed. In contrast, the depleted quality of Anne Elliot's environment is the very subject of *Persuasion*'s opening chapters. The novel foregrounds the unnourishing world of her father and sister and those people, Lady Russell and Mr Shepherd, who do duty as their 'friends'. Elizabeth 'did not quite equal her father in personal contentment', the narrator comments dryly:

> For thirteen years had she been doing the honours, and laying down the domestic law at home, and leading the way to the chaise and four, and walking immediately after Lady Russell out of all the drawing-rooms and dining rooms in the country. Thirteen winters' revolving frosts had seen her opening every ball of credit which a scanty neighbourhood afforded; and thirteen springs shewn their blossoms, as she travelled up to London for a few weeks annual enjoyment of the great world.

Elizabeth 'would have rejoiced to be certain of being properly solicited by baronet-blood within the next twelvemonth or two'. This is Emma's 'what ought to be' seen as self-destructive presumption, pride now examined as self-immolation. While Elizabeth insists on her prerogatives and rights, the seasons perform in mechanical rotation about her, and springs only return to suggest a formal parody of renewed and replenished life. 'Fulfilment' is a Romantic word, but such a term is needed to suggest how Jane Austen associates Elizabeth's spiritual impoverishment, what the narrator calls later 'the sameness . . . and the nothingness' (9) of her life, with the absence of love and emotional satisfaction. Instead she clutches, as does her sister Mary, at every sign of precedence the social world offers her.

Persuasion is, then, a novel about the inner and the outer life. This evocation of the sterility of Elizabeth's social space is a preface to its concern with the outward capability and inner turbulence of the quiet, recessive, and only gradually introduced heroine. Anne is without power in her family circle as she is at first without dramatic prominence in the text, but the narrative becomes gradually suffused with her presence, idioms, and approach. Yet it is through negatives, absences, understatements, merely the cadences and phrasing that shape her introspections, not through an assertive or dramatic voice, that Anne Elliot becomes for the reader a presence in her world.

'Nobody' in her immediate family, she is at least 'useful' in the neighbouring Musgrove circle. There, others talk while she plays the piano. 'She knew that when she played she was giving pleasure only to herself; but this was no new sensation: excepting one short period of her life, she had never, since the age of fourteen, never since the loss of her dear mother, known the happiness of being listened to, or encouraged by any just appreciation or real taste' (47). Such sentences exemplify the way Anne's consciousness is represented in this novel. Defining her solitariness, the sentence, by mentioning the death of her mother, and alluding more indistinctly to the forfeit of Wentworth, manages to suggest the enduring painfulness of both, and how that second loss inscribed the first yet more deeply. The plangent chords of these losses are dwelt on momentarily, but by enclosing, and holding, them within an assertion of Anne's competence, the phrasing also suggests how she has proceeded to a mature, if tenuous, accommodation. Anne's inner life is rendered in touches like this, which open brief perspectives on her emotional and psychological history, on the painful underpinnings of her present condition, but which never dwell on them. Anne's consciousness is imbued with memory and reflection, and the style which evokes it is at once suggestive and understated.

When Captain Wentworth once again enters Anne's life, he thus broaches a tentatively achieved stability. Anne's struggles to come to terms with the momentary encounters and challenges of his presence are represented as moral or ethical struggles to be 'rational' or 'sensible' but also as 'nervous' excitements, physiological responses of energies half repressed but now roused and heightened, in blushes and agitations. Anne Elliot is thus a kind of moral-physiological entity, and the account of her 'reasonings' is accompanied by the continuous registration of a physical state, captured in freer, more agitated prose than Austen has previously developed. Anne's thoughts after their first encounter are presented as a battle, as in a Shakespearian soliloquy, between the counter-vailing forces of desire and self-command, with desire repeatedly infiltrating the pitiful strategems of the stoic will that are marshalled to quell it (60–1). But since Anne's emotional needs are legitimate, the effect of her struggles is to produce a kind of ironic pathos, and the desire of the reader can only be to await their expression and fulfilment. This sense of the intricacy of Anne's psychology—the pull of emotion imperfectly coinciding with conduct; the body, so to speak, shown to have a will of its own, is one of Austen's main achievements in this novel. As an example: unexpectedly discerning Wentworth walking down the street '[S]he now felt a great inclination to go to the outer door; she wanted to see if it rained' (175). Amusingly, Anne provides herself with an excuse for an 'inclination' that is obviously physical desire.

The depth of Anne's solitary consciousness is contrasted with the absence of culture (for Sir Walter picks up no books but the Baronetage) in the life of the surrounding small-time country gentry. The Musgroves are warmhearted and unaffected, unlike the Elliots, but the whole family share an unreflecting philistinism. Finding Charles Hayter with books before him the Musgroves 'were sure all could not be right, and talked, with grave faces, of his studying himself to death' (82). They inhabit a taken-for-granted world, without an inkling that people are not entirely to be known by their appearances, without a glimpse of the pain behind Anne's apparent capability, and quite without insight into their own motives, as for example when Henrietta expresses so much concern for Dr Shirley's health (103–3). When a man she likes talks to her about the value of firmness Louisa Musgrove takes him with her family's literal-mindedness and is resolute at every opportunity, becoming impulsive by rule.

Not even Wentworth or Lady Russell check their own feelings, or distance themselves from them. There is no hint that Lady Russell has felt guilt about the persuasion exerted over Anne in the past—indeed 'her heart revelled in angry pleasure, in pleased contempt' (125) when it appears that her original prejudice about Wentworth is being confirmed—for all the sadness of its consequences. The vehemence of Wentworth's protestation to himself that Anne's 'power with him was gone for ever' (61) suggests, of course, the opposite. But he does not consider this. He is a man of action and energy, trenchant convictions, strong and impulsive feelings that often take him to the verge of tactlessness, but little self-questioning or self-doubt.

Anne Elliot, then, is initially the only reflective consciousness of the novel. (The late-introduced invalid Mrs Smith is perhaps a second.) Isolated within her family, she naturally takes the position of silent observer and is often privately amused at what she sees. Her own perception that she must accommodate to whatever social commonwealth she inhabits sets her always at a slight distance. Like the narrator whose interpretive role she gradually takes over, she is acutely alive to others' self-deceptions, but unlike the narrator, in this book a notably impatient voice, her response is usually kindly. Thus when she plays the piano for the Musgroves she is presented as being happy in their partiality for their daughters' performance over her own, while the writer, on the other hand, caustically suggests that they are 'fond parents' who only '*fancy* themselves delighted' (47: my italics).

Anne's key interpretive role in the narrative is in sharp contrast to what is at first her peripheral place in her social circle. The novel is shaped, indeed, by the way this marginal observer gradually comes to take up a more central position, till in the climactic scene she is the focus of attention in the room. This is paralleled by the way Anne's inner life gradually comes to correspond to, make contact with, and be declared through, the outer life that surrounds her. These processes can be traced in her developing articulacy, for Anne is at first a notably silent observer. Only in Chapter 4 does she become the subject of the narrative, and even then, she does not speak throughout. 'How eloquent could Anne Elliot have been . . . !' declares the author, towards the chapter's close (30). But within the text, Anne is usually eloquent only by indirection or implication. It is with Anne's ears that the reader listens to the many monologues with which this novel defines characters—speeches from Elizabeth, Sir Walter, Mr Shepherd, Mrs Musgrove, Henrietta Musgrove, even Mrs Clay—but what Anne herself says in response is often omitted or absorbed into the meditative commentary of the text. In a telling scene, for example, Lady Russell tempts her with an eloquent vision of herself as Lady Elliot, 'presiding and blessing in the same spot' as her mother (160), and Anne is overcome with such emotion that she must rise and walk to a distant table. But the novel omits her reply. The effect is to suggest that no words can convey the depth of her feeling, and the complexity of her recognition that what she valued in her family life cannot be restored.

Wentworth has made up his mind that he will not speak to Anne. The novel presents a carefully graduated sequence of incidents which bring the two into contact—an intimacy felt acutely in the first instance in bodily terms, as when 'they were actually on the same sofa' (68). Since words are not exchanged, the physical settings in which they meet play an important role. The episode in which her troublesome nephew climbs on Anne's back, for example, is constructed with Anne at the apex of lines of force, or unspoken emotions, in the room, that run between herself and Wentworth, stationed at the window, between Wentworth and Hayter, jealously refusing to speak from behind his newspaper, and between herself and Hayter, who makes one perfunctory attempt to call off his little cousin. The setting is precisely imagined to focus these tensions and to increase them, give them material weight when the little boy hangs himself round Anne's neck (79–80). His unruliness is a metonym for the pressures that are present in the room. Anne has wanted to 'release' Wentworth and herself from embarrassment. Instead the release of the child's 'little sturdy hands' unlocks responses in Anne that are all the more intense because she cannot put them into words. And it is almost as if the boy's unruly attachment to her is an incarnation of Wentworth's still childish rage against, and therefore troublesome and conflicted involvement with, Anne. His release of the boy thus figures as an initial step towards his own release from a psychological blockage.

Another moment of significant progress in their reconciliation occurs after the accident at Lyme. Anne, pausing at the parlour door, overhears Wentworth speaking of her directly. He ought to speak of her politely as 'Miss Anne Elliot', as he speaks of 'Mrs Charles Musgrove', but instead he blurts out 'Anne': 'if Anne will stay, no one so proper, so capable as Anne', for that is the name she goes by in his thoughts. After pausing, she enters the room. "'You will stay, I am sure; you will stay and nurse her"; cried he, turning to her and speaking with a glow, and yet a gentleness, which seemed almost restoring the past' (114). He addresses her as if they were bound to concur—and she is consulted, not merely assumed to be useful. Anne's reply is to 'colour deeply' and her words of acquiescence are, as usual, presented in indirect speech. Characteristically, physical or nervous responses are dramatized, verbal ones are recessed, and if Anne is often silent, her body language speaks volumes. When Wentworth turns to her in the carriage after their silent drive home and asks 'Do you think this a good plan?' Anne's reply is merely presented as 'She did' (117). One is reminded of similar moments of mutual consultation between Emma and Mr Knightley, except that here the traumatic presence of the past is felt, once again, in the inhibition of speech.

The accident at Lyme which concludes Volume I is indeed the turning point both in the relationship of Anne and Wentworth, and in Anne's narrative position. Anne has responded with precisely similar authority to another fall, earlier in the tale (53), but the difference is now that her competence is dramatized and her performance seen by appreciative witnesses. Anne's becoming increasingly an object of regard in her circle is thus paralleled and matched by her increasing presence as a speaker and performer in the text. In Volume II her responses are less elided in the narrative, and more and more fully represented within it. She is less and less confined to the responsive, reactive role (the glances and attentions of Mr Elliot have at least this positive effect). 'My idea of good company, Mr Elliot, is the company of clever, well-informed people, who have a great deal of conversation; that is what I call good company' (150): this assertiveness in his presence is a narrative as well as psychological development. Anne starts declaring her opinions to willing listeners, so that her private thoughts about the Musgrove sisters' impending marriages, for instance, are expressed fully and openly. '"I am extremely glad, indeed", cried Anne' (217); she exclaims that Mr and Mrs Musgrove are excellent parents, she laughs out loud at Musgrove's sketch of Louisa and Benwick's courtship. This development culminates in a dialogue with Harville at the White Hart which is thus as much a formal as an emotional climax to the novel.

Perhaps the novel's greatest achievement is in the choreography of its public or 'crowd' scenes, for it is here that Austen threads her psychological theme through an active and almost picaresque setting, in which hidden motives are up against the exacting pressures of social business. In Bath there is a sense of personal communications having to be made within a crowded, complex world, in continual danger of being thwarted, interrupted or twisted by the projects and emotions of others. Three brilliant social chapters form the novel's climax, the concert in the octagon room (Volume II, Chapter 8) and the gatherings at the Elliots' and Musgroves' apartments (10 and 11). In Chapter 10 Austen succeeds in bringing together almost all of the personages of her novel, giving each of them a characteristic solo turn, and at the same time keeping up the psychological tension and emotional suspense of Anne and Wentworth's relationship. 'A large party in an hotel ensured a quick-changing, unsettled scene' (221).

Serially, a set of incidents occur which bears upon Anne and Wentworth indirectly: Mary's spying Mr Elliot from the window, the squabble of Mary and Charles over the theatre tickets, the chilling visitation of Anne's father and sister to distribute their cards. Elizabeth Bennet had felt that her family conspired to disgrace her, but here the fear that one's projects are continually being trespassed upon, or contaminated, by one's relatives is felt even more acutely. Charles Musgrove's teasing of Mary about their social priorities is more good-natured than Mr Bennet's taunting of his wife, but the significant difference is that the exchange is made to have bearing on the underlying (and quite distinct) drama of Anne and Wentworth's feelings, who extract from it meanings only for themselves.

It is not by chance that Austen sets the climactic scenes of her novel at an inn. This novel is concerned with that distinctively modern form of relation in which bonds are formed between people who are essentially transients. Elective affinities replace and even redeem the lost possibilities of Anne Elliot's emotionally sterile family. In Chapter 11, again at the White Hart, Anne finds herself in the same room with Wentworth. His presence immediately causes a rise in her level of nervous tension. The exchanges of the two principals are once again mediated through a third party, here the overheard conversation of Mrs Musgrove and Mrs Croft, which modulates unexpectedly into a discussion of long engagements. Anne feels 'a nervous thrill all over her' (231). Captain Harville shows the miniature painting of Captain Benwick, once destined for the now dead Fanny Harville, to Anne. The themes of loss and mourning, fidelity and transience, that have occupied so much of Anne Elliot's consciousness in the novel are now resumed and played out dramatically in a conversation. The dialogue begins quietly but rises in seriousness and commitment, as Anne's responses become longer, more assertive, more eloquent. They are momentarily interrupted by a sound in Wentworth's 'hitherto perfectly quiet division of the room' (233), a sound that, punctuating the dialogue, makes one very aware of the spatial relations between the three.

The conversation with Harville resumes, with Anne's contributions once more increasing in length, till both are charged with intense personal feeling. Anne can now speak indirectly, but nonetheless eloquently and fervently, of her personal experience. 'She could not immediately have uttered another sentence; her heart was too full, her breath too much oppressed' (235). Their talk is about love and loyalties sustained over time; in its course Harville and she become friends, as his response indicates: 'You are a good soul', he says while 'putting his hand on her arm quite affectionately'—a wonderfully natural—and modern—touch. The sequence is designed here to release, step by step, the energies of articulation that Anne has been forced to keep bound up, hemmed in, throughout so much of the novel. Thus this climactic scene resolves the tensions that have been kept under in the course of this narrative. Jane Austen has found a way that gives her heroine the initiative, and gives her, finally, the heroine's place. Anne is now at once the woman through whose consciousness the world is seen and organized, and the speaking subject of the text. 'How eloquent could Anne Elliot have been . . . !' Anne's yearning for fulfilment has been codified textually as a longing for expression. Her eloquence at last brings about the resolution of the romantic plot, and leads to the fulfilment of the hero and heroine's desires. At the same time Anne's expressive speech marries together those aspects of her nature that have been so unharmonized with each other throughout the text: feeling and moral action, the responsive body and the responsible self. The design of this novel, only sketched in parts, is effectively complete.

5

Mrs Bennet's Least Favourite Daughter

'In her daughter the mother does not hail a member of the superior caste; in her she seeks a double. She projects upon her daughter all the ambiguity of her relation with herself; and when the otherness of this alter ego manifests itself, the mother feels herself betrayed.'

Simone de Beauvoir, *The Second Sex*

'The aristocracy had also asserted the special character of its body, but this was in the form of blood, that is, in the form of the antiquity of its ancestry and of the value of its alliances; the bourgeoisie on the contrary looked to its progeny and the health of its organism when it laid claim to a specific body. The bourgeoisie's "blood" was its sex.'

Michel Foucault, *The History of Sexuality*, Volume I

Most readers and critics, quite rightly, think of *Pride and Prejudice* as a love story, the romance of Elizabeth Bennet and Fitzwilliam Darcy. Its special quality as a romantic narrative, as Roger Gard puts it, is that the obstacles to the lovers' fulfilment are 'psychological and internal, not a matter of external bars'.[1] Encountering each other at first with antagonism, the two main figures must pass through this misunderstanding, work through their initial mistakes until they recognise their feelings (and each other) for what they are. Austen's work then is illuminated by Jessica Benjamin's contention that recognition of the other person's uniqueness is a rare potential of the psyche, a release from the otherwise ubiquitous 'bonds of love'.[2] Similar reasoning, focused on the central couple, leads the philosopher Slavoj Zizek to suggest that Austen is a novelist who is comparable in stature to Hegel as a thinker. Imagining as 'a comical hypothesis' that 'the first encounter of the future lovers was a success—that Elizabeth had accepted Darcy's proposal', he asks:

What would happen? Instead of being bound together in true love, they would become a vulgar everyday couple, a liaison of an arrogant, rich man and a pretentious, empty-headed young girl. If we want to spare ourselves the painful roundabout route through the misrecognition, we miss the Truth itself: only the 'working through' of the misrecognition allows us to accede to the true nature of the other and at the same time to overcome our own deficiency.[3]

It can certainly be claimed then, that the central relation of the novel is not only an alluring romance, but a profound account—at once epistemological and psychological—of the meaning of love.

But it is not quite true to say that the obstacles to the love of Darcy and Elizabeth are internal rather than external, nor quite just to the novel to treat the ethical and personal drama of their relation as the exclusive focus of the text. The character who illustrates this most clearly is Mrs Bennet, and in this chapter I shall focus on this figure, whose relation to her second daughter has not received extensive critical attention— surprisingly little, considering the dominant position she has in the first chapters of the novel, the important role she plays in her daughter's fate, and—as I shall suggest—the rather profound and disconcerting kinds of dramatic implication that Austen succeeds in generating around her. Mrs Bennet, though, is not easy to think about: and to dismiss her is perhaps, after all, only to defend oneself against her.

For one common approach to the character is to consider it as a caricature, of which *Pride and Prejudice* contains several, including Mr Collins—as a figure somehow beyond the pale, whom we need not take seriously. What might justify this treatment? On the first page of *Pride and Prejudice*, writes Julia Prewitt Brown, 'we have only the disembodied voices of wife and husband clashing in an empty space'.[4] D.W. Harding notes too this 'stageyness of technique' and suggests that '[t]he influence of the eighteenth-century theatre in some parts of the novel is consistent with the very strongly marked caricature of some figures and a rather sharp transition from them to the seriously portrayed characters'.[5] A caricature, roughly speaking, is a figure which does not interact with others and thus does not develop, does not deepen in interest to the reader, but merely goes on displaying the same traits in different circumstances—the amusement to be gained from such figures being in the nature of the running joke. Mrs Bennet's references to her 'nerves', for instance, would certainly put her in this category.

Pride and Prejudice, famously, was 'lopt & cropt'.[6] This casual reference in Jane Austen's letter on receiving her first copy of the novel is probably an allusion to Sheridan's *The Critic*.[7] There are aspects of Mrs Bennet which do suggest the influence of that eighteenth-century theatre with which Austen, from her girlhood, was most certainly familiar.[8] The Bennets' relationship, for example, has its precursors in such couples as the Oaklys in George Colman's much performed *The Jealous Wife* (1761). When thwarted or baffled, Mrs Oakly, like Mrs Bennet, uses her body and illness symptoms in comically unavailing attempts to get her own way. The same play can illustrate that staple of the comic theatre, the self-contradictory speech, as when the heroine Harriot's father blusters 'But she shall have him: I will make her happy, if I break her heart for it.' The speech of Sir Antony Absolute in Sheridan's *The Rivals*, (1775: performed at Steventon in 1784) is full of similar moments: 'So you will fly out! can't you be cool, like me? What the devil good can Passion do!—Passion is of no service, you impudent, insolent, over-bearing Reprobate!—There you sneer again!—don't provoke me!—but you rely upon the mildness of my temper—you do, you Dog! you play upon the meekness of my disposition!' The absurdly contradictory and self-undermining speech is a comic form adopted wholeheartedly by Austen and examples can be found in all her novels. 'What is your opinion now of this sad business of Jane's', asks Mrs Bennet of Elizabeth, 'For my part, I am determined never to speak of it again to anybody. I told my sister Philips so the other day' (227). 'I told you in the library, you know', she has earlier harangued Elizabeth, 'that I should never speak to you again, and you will find me as good as your word. I have no pleasure in talking to undutiful children.— Not that I have much pleasure indeed in talking to any body. People who suffer as I do from nervous complaints can have no great inclination for talking. Nobody can tell what I suffer!— But it is always so. Those who do not complain are never pitied.' (113)

What distinguishes an effusion like this (and its inevitable follow-up 'all of you, hold your tongues, and let Mr Collins and me have a little conversation together' (113)) from the comic display of the theatre is the presence of Mrs Bennet's daughters and the demands, partly stated, partly implied, such behaviour makes on them. It is thus not possible merely to dismiss Mrs Bennet as a fool, because the focus of the reader's attention is at least in part on the cost she exacts from those who have to spend their days listening to her. If the reader feels both amusement and contempt at this figure's mindless inanities he or she must also reflect that despising one's mother is a far from comfortable position for a daughter, especially an extremely intelligent daughter, to be in.

'Silences in *Pride and Prejudice*', comments Tara Ghoshal Wallace, 'are never neutral.'[9] We might well imagine Elizabeth Bennet listening to her mother at such moments, or sitting through such a shameless speech as that at Netherfield in which she attempts to market Jane to Bingley and thinking 'This woman is a caricature. She's grotesque. *And what's more, she's my mother.*' Mrs Bennet, then, would no longer belong to a closed sphere of narrative convention when brought into relation with a heroine with whom the reader has already formed a sympathetic bond. But no such thought, of course, appears in the text. 'The mother was found to be intolerable' by Miss Bingley and Mrs Hurst; Darcy, with due regard to the pain he is giving, reminds Elizabeth of the 'total want of propriety' of her mother's behaviour; but Elizabeth's thoughts about her mother are never presented in the articulate form I have imagined them. 'The circumstances to which he particularly alluded, as having passed at the Netherfield ball . . . could not have made a stronger impression on his mind than on hers', the reader is told as Elizabeth reviews Darcy's letter. Elizabeth had certainly 'blushed and blushed again with shame and vexation' at her mother's domination of the conversation on that occasion. Mortified, embarrassed, though she most definitely is, her responses to her mother never take the articulate and formulated shape that she allows herself in criticism of her father. Never neutral, the silence of Elizabeth about her relation to her mother is charged with potent implications.

Wallace comments too on that memorable moment at Netherfield in which Elizabeth is attempting to keep up a polite conversation about the comparative merits of life in town and country, saying 'But people themselves alter so much, that there is something new to be observed in them for ever', and Mrs Bennet unexpectedly 'cries' 'Yes, indeed . . . I assure you there is quite as much of *that* going on in the country as in town.' 'Everybody was surprised; and Darcy, after looking at her for a moment, turned silently away' (43). As Wallace notes, the text offers 'no explanation as to why this innocuous inanity should give rise to so much surprise, silence and triumph' (45). What on earth is she saying? The hiccup in the conversation opens a gap which can only be filled by her listeners' and the reader's imagination. Thomas R. Edwards comments that 'Austen draws scenes of embarrassment that seem to point not towards morally instructive shame but towards a realm of feelings that are too strong or dangerous for even Austen's powers of irony and discernment to deal with securely'.[10] Perhaps this is one. Using the same turn of phrase, Mrs Norris' implication in the opening pages of *Mansfield Park* is unmistakable: 'You are thinking of your sons— but do not you know that of all things upon earth *that* is the least likely to happen; brought up as they would be, always together like brothers and sisters?' (*MP* 6). Though hardly understanding what is being said in this carefully managed polite argument, Mrs Bennet thrusts herself forward in her daughter's place, and thus uncovers to the listening group the force of her egotism, and even of something that might be obscurely felt as her brute desire.[11] But the work of interpreting the silence that follows her remark, or the nature of her 'triumph' in causing it, is certainly devolved upon the reader.

Mrs Bennet has an intrusive, an almost physical presence in these first chapters of *Pride and Prejudice*, and this effect is accomplished without any description of her person. As in this instance, the reader experiences her repeatedly as overriding, or taking possession of her daughters' lives.[12] On her first appearance in the novel, for example, Elizabeth Bennet's speech is usurped by her mother. 'Observing his second daughter employed in trimming a hat', Mr Bennet suddenly says to her, 'I hope Mr Bingley will like it Lizzy'. 'We are not in a way to know what Mr Bingley likes', said her mother resentfully, 'since we are not to visit'(6). Taking over Elizabeth's right of reply, she simultaneously displays herself as sulky, rude and resentful. Yet, of course, if there is an ugly form of symbiosis in Mrs Bennet's relation to her daughters (exemplified a moment later in a different mode when, 'unable to contain herself', she attempts to dictate when Kitty shall cough), the novel offers plenty of extenuating circumstances. It is entirely natural and plausible that a mother in her situation, with a feckless, unprovident husband and five daughters, would develop an overriding anxiety about their future, and fail to honour the distinctiveness of their natures and destinies from her own.

Moreover in this small scene she is caught in one of her husband's habitual conversational traps. In addressing his daughter in preference to his wife, Mr Bennet is by implication displacing his wife, and favouring Elizabeth with the attention and information he knows she craves. But though *Pride and Prejudice* clearly (and explicitly) suggests that Mr Bennet has a lot to answer for, the overriding implication, I think, is not that, having regard to their economic circumstances Mrs Bennet's psychology is one we can, at a stretch, sympathise with and understand. Instead—and fostered by the narration's close affinity with Elizabeth's point of view—it is to force upon the reader, repeatedly, scenes in which Mrs Bennet's talk and behaviour are felt to be personally offensive, in all nuances of the word. Though the role of mother is certainly the only one her society allows her to claim, she is that worst exemplar of the mother, a woman who cannot separate herself from her offspring because she is in many respects herself still an envious and fractious child.

Mrs Bennet, then, to use the phrase Austen repeatedly attaches to her, is 'unable to contain herself'. Of demonstrably 'uncertain temper', her fluctuations of mood have no fulcrum, no internal resting place. From 'lamentation' to 'transport' her emotional oscillations are extreme. Mr Bennet's announcement that he has visited Bingley after all is greeted by a 'tumult of joy': he leaves the room, 'fatigued by her raptures'. When she is thwarted, she is resentful and childish, declares herself 'nervous and poorly', and is prone to express her disappointments in an array of real or imagined physical symptoms. Her world is black and white: Bingley is excessively handsome and his sisters are charming women; Darcy, on the contrary is shockingly rude and a most disagreeable, horrid man. She is undoubtedly funny, too: but there is something else about Mrs Bennet that makes her disturbing. It is that we glimpse, in the violence of her emotions, in the volubility of her discourse, in the unnuanced, coarse vibrations of her presence, a great deal of energy. And it is sexual energy, too. 'I remember the time when I liked a red coat very well—and indeed so I do still at my heart' (29): this confession, early in the novel, already indicates how Mrs Bennet's still unappeased sexuality is to play its role in fostering her youngest daughter's erotic escapade. Thus, in another demonstration of her failure to keep her own life and emotions separate from her daughters', Mrs Bennet later champions Lydia's desire to go to Brighton in terms of her own wishes. 'A little sea bathing would set me up for ever'(229) she opines. Her husband, of course, is implicated too: I imagine that Mr Bennet, so practised at closing his study door, is practised too at turning his back in bed.

The sexuality of a mother is not a pretty spectacle to her daughters, even when it is buried, as here, represented only as erratic forays, hypochondria and hysterics. But the text has another secret to disclose, even more disturbing. Jane receives a note from Netherfield. 'Mrs Bennet's eyes sparkled with pleasure, and she was eagerly calling out while her daughter read, "Well, Jane, who is it from, and what is it about? What does he say? Well, Jane, make haste and tell us; make haste, my love"' (30). It is not just her inquisitiveness, nor the assumption in her questions that the correspondent must be Bingley—both signals of her overbearing possessiveness—that is telling here. Soon, Mr Bennet, relishing the mystery he is creating, tells his wife and daughters that he is expecting an addition to the family party. '"The person of whom I speak, is a gentleman and a stranger." Mrs Bennet's eyes sparkled.— "A gentleman and a stranger! It is Mr Bingley I am sure"' (61). No other indication of Mrs Bennet as a physical being is given except her 'sparkling eyes'. And this notation occurs in the midst of chapters in which her second daughter's 'fine eyes' (27) catch the attention of Darcy, and are repeatedly kept before the reader by the tiresome and unavailing teasing of him by Miss Bingley (36, 46). Can this similarity of notation be an accident? Or is it the signal of a consanguinity that the text elsewhere deploys in a more veiled form? Are Mrs Bennet's baffled energies a distorted, bizarre version of her daughter's transgressive high spirits—this daughter who runs everywhere? Elizabeth's provocative social manner remains within the wiry bounding line of decorum, but it surely reproduces, in moderated form, her mother's forwardness. Is Mrs Bennet's embodiment then a more or less pathological variation of her daughter's vitality? One does not press such questions too far. Yet we can begin to see how Austen prompts the reader's imagination to fill in the spaces, the silences of the relation between Elizabeth and her mother. Even Mrs Bennet's comic self-contradictions are echoed, to provide a more subtle amusement for the reader, when Elizabeth tells her mother that she can 'safely promise . . . *never* to dance with' Darcy. (20)

Another set of links between Mrs Bennet and her 'least dear' daughter is routed through her favourite daughter, Lydia. Neglected, left to her own devices, Lydia plainly replicates the narcissism and thoughtlessness of her mother, for whom she is an alter-ego, the re-enactment of her youth.[13] Like her, she is forward and shameless. 'Untamed, unabashed, wild, noisy and fearless' (315), Lydia's forward sexuality is a caricature of everything the novel communicates about its heroine, but keeps implicit. Like her mother, Lydia, then, is a comedic figure who at the same time relates seriously to the heroine's romantic life. Elizabeth, 'headstrong' and 'wild', as Mrs Bennet calls her, confounds her mother, because this daughter's presence, her status with the father, her wit's access to a realm of meaning forever out of her ken, stands as a constant reminder of something which cannot be governed or appropriated. When Miss Bingley calls Elizabeth 'almost wild' after her walk across the fields and stiles to Netherfield it is interesting that this comment is followed closely by Darcy's reiteration of his 'admiration' of her eyes: 'they were brightened by the exercise' (36). The short pause which follows this speech is analogous to the pause after Mrs Bennet's interruption: it allows space in which the reader understands the unconscious message contained in this conjunction. Wildness, bright eyes and physical vitality come together in one intensely alluring and potentially very disruptive package. Like Lydia, Elizabeth is a force, her energy capable, as the novel demonstrates, of altering the world. Both are forward and self confident. More disconcertingly, both enjoy a laugh.

Elizabeth is ashamed to think that, though she would never speak as vulgarly as Lydia does about the looks of Wickham's temporary conquest, Mary King, she has had the same illiberal thought that only Miss King's money could have attracted him. Perhaps Elizabeth is incapable of 'coarseness of expression' about Miss King but there is another rival in the novel about whom she certainly has similarly snide, even coarse, thoughts. 'Only look at her. She is quite a little creature. Who would have thought she could be so thin and small!' This is Maria Lucas's comment on Miss Anne de Bourgh. '"I like her appearance", said Elizabeth, struck with other ideas. "She looks sickly and cross.—Yes, she will do for him very well. She will make him a very proper wife."' Superficially this serves to keep before the reader Elizabeth's still-lingering interest in Darcy. Yet the novel reiterates Elizabeth's malice when she is actually introduced to the heiress at Rosings. She 'could almost have joined in Maria's astonishment at her being so thin and so small . . . Miss De Bourgh was pale and sickly; her features, though not plain, were insignificant . . .' (145). Why is Elizabeth at this moment given such a petty, even vulgar thought? In so economical a text, a text which leaves so much to the reader's intuition, this redundant emphasis on the 'sickliness' of the heroine's rival is intriguing. For Miss Anne has no other role in the novel than to be the opposite of Elizabeth Bennet.

Foucault's distinction between the 'blood' of the aristocracy—a matter of lineage—and the 'blood' of the bourgeois—a matter of healthy sexual vitality—might throw some light on this. It's a commonplace of Austen criticism that *Persuasion* commemorates, or celebrates, the accession to political and social power of a new social class—or rather the recruitment into the gentry of the energies and enterprise of a group previously marginalised. The same pattern is clearly at work in *Pride and Prejudice*. In other words, this novel too (seen in this sociological and historicist framework) is about the recruitment of energies, the replenishment by 'new blood', and thus the perpetuation, of the higher realms of the landed gentry. Elizabeth belongs inevitably to the 'bourgeois' world her mother and her sister Lydia body forth: their rampant and violent energy is only the coarsest sign of that sexual vitality that, as well as her freedom from mere convention, has drawn the eye of the 'aristocratic' Darcy, and that she brings to the marriage. Thus the novel in celebrating the marriage of this young woman to this rich man—a marriage that 'pollutes' the pure blood of Pemberley—is avowing (I think unconsciously) its solidarity with the dynamic forces her mother and sister represent.

I have been arguing then, that Mrs Bennet affects the reader more deeply than a caricature could ever do, that whilst still being grotesque, she is not dismissable as an independent ingredient in a novel concerned mainly with her daughter's romance. Obviously Mrs Bennet's habitual impropriety is a material impediment to her daughter's chances of making a prosperous marriage. But the novel is portraying something more intimate, more potent in the relation of mother and daughter. When the mother is felt to be uncomfortably close to the self, the dream of escape from her is all the more urgent. Thinking about Mrs Bennet leads one to conclude that *Pride and Prejudice* retains its hold as a great romantic narrative, not just because it tells the story of Darcy and Elizabeth's quarrel and reconcilement, but because it enacts in the boldest and most persuasive form the young adult's desire for differentiation and separation from the parent of the same sex.

Mrs Bennet, shameless herself, reduces her witty, outgoing daughter to agonies of shame. She is a monstrous announcement of that experience almost every young person endures, some time or other, in the presence of their parents. From this psychological fund the novel draws when it invites the reader to understand that Mrs Bennet, though comical (and perhaps never so comical as when the news of Elizabeth's engagement to Darcy reduces her, for once, to cataleptic silence), is simultaneously, in the volatility of her temperament, in the illiberality of her mind, in the pushy materialism of her ambitions, a persistent shadow over her daughter's destiny. That is why the fact that Pemberley is so far from Longbourn is made much of. It is stressed too that the Gardiners—the surrogate father and mother—come and visit, but it is Elizabeth's triumph that in loving and marrying Darcy, she succeeds in escaping from, and in putting so much distance between, herself and Mrs Bennet, her mother.

6

Editing *Mansfield Park*

When I was first asked to edit *Mansfield Park* for the forthcoming Cambridge Edition of the Works of Jane Austen I was told rather breezily that I would probably find a copy of the original edition in my local public library. When I got back to Melbourne I discovered that there were in fact only two copies of the first edition of *Mansfield Park* in the whole of Australia, and not one of the second edition of 1816. This was not, in retrospect, though, altogether surprising. The novel was first published in 1814 by Thomas Egerton, who had made a killing with *Pride and Prejudice* the previous year, and then, when he seems to have declined to take on a second edition, by John Murray in February 1816. The first edition of *Mansfield Park* was of perhaps 1250 copies, the second of 750. The first had sold out by November 1814: the second found little more than 250 buyers, and 'was in fact remaindered' in 1820.[1] No wonder then, that there were so few copies of either edition in a place as far away as Australia.

That *Mansfield Park* exists in two editions makes much of the interest and challenge of editing the text. (The MS, needless to say, has not survived.) It was this second edition that I was instructed to take as my 'copy' or 'base' text. This is a controversial decision, since the orthodoxy of contemporary bibliographical theory favours the first edition of works, understood to be closer to the author's original manuscript.

All texts will have been subjected to the interventions and errors, the manipulations and misconstruings of publisher's readers (where they existed) and typesetters or compositors, but it is believed that there will be less of these in first editions, than in subsequent ones. Thus one can plausibly argue that the earliest edition resembles the author's original intention more closely than later ones, even when the author has had subsequent access to the text.

All later publications of *Mansfield Park*, though, with one notable exception, have taken the second edition—more or less—as their basis. In December 1815 we have a note from Jane Austen to John Murray written from her brother Henry's London home, 23 Hans Place, thanking him for the loan of books and saying that 'I return also, *Mansfield Park*, as ready for a 2nd Edit: I believe, as I can make it', which seems fairly strong authority for the assumption that Austen herself had a hand in the changes that mark the novel's republishing. All of the nineteenth century reprints I have examined follow this 1816 edition, and it was also 'in the main', as he put it, the basis for R.W. Chapman's great Clarendon edition of 1923— by far the most important in the history of Austen republication, deeply influential, and itself in turn the basis for almost all reprints of the novel since. 'The Text based on Collation of the Early Editions' proudly announces the title page of Chapman's *Austen*. The Dent edition, edited by R. Brimley Johnson, in 1892, had noted places where its text deviated from the 1816 original, but Chapman's was the first, and till recently the only, edition that went back to the earliest texts, compared them, and (at least in many instances) showed readers the differences between the two versions. His work remains something of a challenge and a provocation to all subsequent editors, but his editions are now manifestly out of date.

One can interpret Austen's message to Murray, though, in a variety of ways: in some moods I think we should take the phrasing very seriously (after all this is a formal letter, on the record, so to speak) and that Austen is here writing as the professional (or quasi-professional) author, and that the last phrase means exactly what it says. In other moods I think that it's a mistake to project our own standards of editing and copy-editing onto Austen, and that it may be an ahistorical view of the importance of the novel that leads us to imagine that people in the past, even its author, took the details of its presentation with the seriousness we do. At the climax of the first volume, for instance, in the midst of the rehearsals for *Lovers' Vows*, both the 1814 and the 1816 editions tell us that the company were 'too much engaged in their own noise, to be struck by an usual noise in the other part of the house'. In conformity with the contemporary ethics of editorial practice, Claudia Johnson, in her recent edition of the novel for Norton adopts and defends this reading,[2] but I can't see that it makes any sense: what is the point of saying, unidiomatically, 'an usual noise' when the normal form 'a noise' implies it just as well? Why should they have been 'struck' by ordinary noise? Chapman and all other subsequent editors emend this either to 'an unusual', or just 'unusual' (which certainly sounds better). Surely a conscientious and attentive reader, looking over her own text for a second edition, such as we imagine Austen would have been, might have picked up this error? (But then we know authors read what they think they have put there.) This is a good example of the sort of mistake that might be missed in the printing house, though, since texts were read aloud for checking, often by boys who would not understand the sense of what they were reading.[3] Read rapidly aloud as it would have been, the incorrect 'an usual' is easily misheard, and therefore passed, as the correct 'unusual'.

So I have had to shift the focus from our own sense of *Mansfield Park* as a very serious, highly accomplished work of art, a classic, and peer down into that undergrowth of literature in which this now-prized specimen originally grew. It is no exaggeration to speak of the novel as the bottom end of the publishing market: 'novel trash' was the phrase that sprang most readily to contemporaries' lips.[4] This is easily demonstrated by the prices publishers paid their authors. Leaving aside such famous persons as Frances Burney and Maria Edgeworth—the best paid authoress of the age—the impoverished gentlewoman who mostly supplied the novel market rarely made more than a hundred or so pounds for each work.[5] We remember that *Susan*, the precursor of *Northanger Abbey*, for instance, was sold in 1803 for £10. *Sense and Sensibility* was published by Austen herself 'on commission', meaning that she, not the publisher, took the risk of that novel's failure. Following its success, Egerton paid Austen £110 for the copyright of *Pride and Prejudice*, the same sum that in the same years John Murray was paying Robert Southey for each essay he contributed to the *Quarterly Review*. But then, novels were rarely printed in runs of more than 1,000, and the *Quarterly* by this time was selling over 7,000, and taken by every Tory family in the land (the Rushworths at Sotherton were thus typical). Like *Sense and Sensibility*, *Mansfield Park* had been published by Egerton on the author's commission—so that, in effect, Austen might well have lost, rather than made, money on it.

The *Mansfield Park* of 1814, then, is a product, like Austen's others, destined in large part, for the circulating library market. By this time established in all towns, large and small (Fanny Price herself subscribes to one in Portsmouth), they included a high proportion of novels in their stock, something like 40%. Novels, almost always published in several volumes, were borrowed by the volume, differing rates entitling a subscriber to one or more at a time. These libraries, not individuals, were the chief purchasers of new novels. It is usually suggested that the circulating libraries would have taken at least three or four hundred of a new production likely to appeal to their readers.[6] Since *Pride and Prejudice* had undoubtedly been a success, and Egerton had published a second edition (it is advertised at the back of his issue of *Mansfield Park*), the advance orders for *Mansfield Park* are likely to have been on the high side. As well as the circulating libraries there were many non-commercial book clubs too (Austen belonged to one in Chawton): and these might also order any successful new novel.

Three volume novels were the pulp fiction of the day, the 'trash with which the press now groans' in Wordworth's phrase (and when many presses were still wood, the groaning was real—hence the associated metaphor of giving birth). If the term 'trash' was always applied to them, this was partly because, everyone agreed, their shelf-life at the circulating library was short, three months, if you were lucky: and those unsold, then as now, were remaindered or pulped. These were objects to be consumed, read and disposed of. But they were not cheap. A work like *Mansfield Park* cost 18 shillings for the three volumes. This, multiplied by 40, the commonly accepted ratio, is about the same as the current price for an academic monograph in hard-back—a species that has been called the career library book. As the proprietors of circulating libraries advertised, you could borrow and read an awful lot of novels for less than that sum. You did not expect to re-read a novel, so the ordinary gentleman or lady with a modest income rarely bought them.[7] For the same amount you could borrow many from the local library and return them often, like Mary Musgrove in *Persuasion* (Volume II, Chapter 2).

Thus, in November 1814 we find Jane Austen writing to her niece Fanny Knight about the future of *Mansfield Park*. 'It is not yet settled whether I *do* hazard a 2nd Edition.—People are more ready to borrow & praise, than to buy—which I cannot wonder at.'[8] Publication on commission is obviously the arrangement envisaged for another edition; a risk, as Austen intimates, even for a novel that has sold out in its first, and made the author a handsome sum (calculated to be more than £310).[9] But negotiations with Egerton seem to have broken down. Deirdre Le Faye's revision of the 1913 *Life and Letters of Jane Austen*, published as *A Family Record*, speaks of Egerton's 'refusal' to bring out a second edition:[10] but it is not clear what went on. Only fragments of letters survive for the months between November 1814 and September 1815. Nor is it clear how or why a decision was made to approach Murray, or whether perhaps Murray approached Austen. But on 17 October 1815 Austen is writing to Cassandra that 'Mr Murray's letter is come; he is a Rogue of course, but a civil one. He offers £450 [for *Emma*]—but wants to have the Copyright of *MP*, & *S&S* included. It will end in my publishing for myself I dare say.'[11] So Murray published *Emma* (1815), in an edition of 2000 copies, but on commission, and a second edition of *Mansfield Park* on the same arrangement—Henry Austen, on Austen's behalf, having refused his original offer.[12]

Murray's adoption of Austen is an important moment in the history of her novels and their reputation. His agreeing to republish *Mansfield Park* has special and I believe, under-appreciated significance. Circulating library copies were bound in marble boards, instantly recognisable as the cheapest form of binding. (Mr Collins 'started back' on beholding the book the Bennet sisters produce for him to read aloud, 'for every thing announced it to be from a circulating library' (Volume I, Chapter 4)). Presumably some copies would have been worn out and in need of replacement if demand for a certain novel continued. But 'the rage was for new books immediately upon publication'.[13] It is unlikely that the publishers of a second edition of a novel would have anything like the numbers of orders for it that they routinely took for the first. I think therefore that when the second edition of a novel is published, it is because it can be sold to private buyers. What this means, in turn, is that the novel is understood to bear, or invite, re-reading. It is not just trash—real or potential. What we have here then, I might further venture, is the incipient moment, the very beginnings, of 'canon formation'.[14]

Murray (actually John Murray II) had taken over his father's business in 1803. By 1815 he was firmly established as the most prestigious of London publishers, the proprietor of the *Quarterly Review* (started in 1809) with connections in the Cabinet and a 'stable' of important writers. His library and drawing room at Albemarle Street became the centre of literary London. (There, on 9 April 1815, occurred, for instance, the famous meeting between his two best-selling and most famous authors, Lord Byron and Walter Scott.) John Murray published few novels, apart from Scott's, already a best-selling poet, though he had floated the idea of a series of 'British Novelists', to include Richardson and Fielding, but also Burney and Charlotte Smith, in 1808. Austen's accession to Murray's list is a vital moment in her elevation to canonical status: she joins Scott, Southey, Byron and many others sharing broadly Tory political principles (though as a good business man, Murray did not allow politics altogether to dictate what he published.) During these same months Austen receives the invitation to dedicate *Emma* to the Prince Regent: it is the moment when this lady author from Hampshire is being drawn or received into the conservative literary establishment.

Murray's chief reader (the role was unofficial at the time— and a secret) was William Gifford, the editor of the *Quarterly Review*. As part of the negotiations it would seem that Murray passed on a copy of *Pride and Prejudice* to him (perhaps Murray might have some idea of buying the copyright from Egerton). Extracts from a couple of Gifford's letters to Murray were printed for the first time in Samuel Smiles's *A Publisher and His Friends* (1891) and though brief, they are illuminating. In the first Gifford says he has read the novel, which is 'really a very pretty thing'. On 29 September 1815 he writes 'I have read *Pride and Prejudice again*—'tis very good—wretchedly printed, and so pointed as to be almost unintelligible. . . .' The underlining of '*again*' is significant. After all, one does not usually read novels twice: they are not of a nature to demand re-reading.[15] So Gifford is saying, in effect: 'This is a novel people would want to have: it deserves to be printed well.' Jane Austen herself commented upon the 'Typical errors' in the setting of her text.[16] But Gifford's letter is before we hear any whisper on Austen's side of negotiations with Murray. On the same day as his letter was written, she writes from Chawton that she is soon 'going to London for a week or two': there, at Henry's, she carried on those negotiations for the publication of *Emma* that entailed the re-publication of *Mansfield Park*.

Gifford goes on to suggest that he might help with the editing of *Emma*. This might imply that the printers of Murray's editions of Austen were to give especial attention to 'pointing', so as to render justice to these singularly valuable novels. The printing of Egerton's *Mansfield Park* is certainly equally as wretched as that of *Pride and Prejudice*, especially in the first volume. Chapman says it is 'by far the worst printed' of Austen's novels.[17] But how many of the changes in the second edition are to be attributed to Austen herself, and how many to the attentions of Murray's reader (if there were one) and type-setters? In other words, is the first or the second edition closer to what Austen herself wrote? Are we now reading Austen's text through a layer of incrustations imposed on it by printers and publishers concerned to make the text conform to their conceptions of a standard—standards possibly quite different from the author's own? But she seems to have accepted, at least, that her own spelling might be eccentric: having joked about a 'modest query' of the compositor against her spelling of '*arra*-root' in *Emma*, she does go on in the same letter to spell the word correctly.[18]

The problem of which edition is the best confronts the editor of *Mansfield Park* with the novel's very first sentence. In 1814 this began:

About thirty years ago, Miss Maria Ward, of Huntingdon, with only seven thousand pounds, had the good luck to captivate Sir Thomas Bertram, of Mansfield Park, in the county of Northampton. . . .

In 1816 it read:

About thirty years ago, Miss Maria Ward of Huntingdon, with only seven thousand pounds, had the good luck to captivate Sir Thomas Bertram, of Mansfield Park, in the county of Northampton. . . .

Perhaps—one might argue—it was a perception of the false parallelism between coming from Huntingdon and having the proud address of 'Mansfield Park, in the county of Northampton' that led someone to delete the comma after 'Ward'. This someone might be Jane Austen, or the typesetter. On the other hand, it might be suggested that the parallel is ironic: putting the two addresses in tandem sharpens a perception of the good luck inherent in Miss Ward's elevation. This would make the deletion of the comma almost certainly the printer's. But since almost all of the amendments to punctuation in the second edition consist of additions, I am inclined to think that this is Austen's emendation: one would hardly expect a typesetter, beginning the novel, to interfere with what is, on the face of it, an entirely regular bit of pointing.

So I would argue that Austen herself did pay close attention to the printed text of the first edition, and amended it carefully. Chapman suggests that she corrected a copy of the first edition, not the MS or a fair copy in her own hand-writing, and I'm sure he's right: it is certainly clear from the 1816 edition that the typesetter followed the setting out of a 1814 copy, only varying to give better spacing, or to set out dialogue correctly.[19] So—for instance—Austen amended naval details in the third volume, and added a needed 'however' to the novel's second paragraph that quickly clarifies the sequence of events. When the thirteen-year old Maria is boasting to Mrs Norris of her educational attainments, and running down Fanny in the process ('How long ago it is, aunt, since we used to repeat the chronological order of the kings of England . . . !') both marking off the address to the aunt by commas, and the exclamation mark are additions made in the second edition. This exclamation mark, like the ellipsis that is added to Fanny's struggles to say something nice about Mary Crawford in Volume I, Chapter 16 ('"She was most kind indeed, and I am glad to have her spared" . . . She could not finish the generous effusion.') are refinements of the author, sharpening what is already present in her characters' speech.

Chapman, using the second edition as his copy-text, assumed that Austen herself made most of these changes in punctuation. But Chapman, sympathetic and informed, was also eclectic: when he thought the reading of the first edition was better, he used this rather than the second. Sometimes he noted this, sometimes he didn't. An illuminating example of his practice comes in the first chapter of *Mansfield Park*, where in 1816 we read: '"Then she had better come to us?" said Lady Bertram.' In his Notes to his edition Chapman comments 'Lady Bertram seldom asks questions', in justification of his text's reversion here to the first edition's 'to us'. But quite apart from the question of editorial principles (not enunciated with their present severity in Chapman's day) the assumption is questionable. In fact, Lady Bertram often asks questions. 'What is the play about, Fanny, you have never told me?' (Volume I, Chapter 13). 'What shall I do, Sir Thomas?—Whist and Speculation; which will amuse me most?' (Volume II, Chapter 7). Lady Bertram is often said to 'observe', and the observation follows with a question mark: 'Lady Bertram soon brought the matter to a head, by carelessly observing to Mrs Norris,—"I think, sister, we need not keep Miss Lee any longer, when Fanny goes to live with you?" The conjunction of a question mark with 'said', as at the opening of (Volume II, Chapter 5), '"But why should Mrs Grant ask Fanny?" said Lady Bertram', is in fact the text's representation of her combined amenableness, indolence and incuriosity. If the case were reversed, and it was the first edition that had the question mark, then one could certainly assume that the second edition bore the sign of authorial correction of a printer's error. But if you ask me, I would say that the apparent oddity of the conjunction of the syntax of a statement with the pointing of a question mark in the second edition is evidence of Jane Austen's own attention to the minutiae of her text, an idiosyncrasy of her style, a deft characterising invention, that she wished to instate, or reinstate, in defiance of convention.

A case could be made, then, for sticking to the second edition, more rigorously than Chapman. Most of the changes are of the kind that a practised editor like Gifford might introduce: the occasional substitution of a colon for a semi-colon, dependent clauses marked off by commas—that sort of thing. Thus Edmund's comment on Shakespeare in 1814 is 'To know him in bits and scraps, is common enough, to know him pretty thoroughly, is perhaps not uncommon, but to read him well aloud, is no everyday talent.' In 1816, his speech has been repunctuated: 'To know him in bits and scraps, is common enough; to know him pretty thoroughly, is, perhaps, not uncommon; but to read him well aloud, is no every-day talent.' Whether this application of rigorous pointing to a speech already pompous enough, is an improvement is debatable. Perhaps Gifford or someone of that ilk supplied it, perhaps the typesetter, to whom authors were often content to leave their work, perhaps Austen herself. Punctuative intensity is not confined to the 1816 edition. Mary Crawford on Tom: '*He* had been much in London, and had more liveliness than Edmund, and must, therefore, be preferred; and, indeed, his being the eldest was another strong claim.' Here, the pointing—the same in both editions—is a form of synecdoche or metonymy: it captures Mary's 'official' thoughts about Tom, whilst leaving it open as to whether there might not be an unofficial self with other leanings. In instances like this we can see, I believe, that Austen harnesses the possibilities of punctuating the language (the dramatic possibilities of rhythm) much as a poet does.

As I have said, all current editions of *Mansfield Park*—there have been four new editions in the last ten years—are based on, and indebted to, Chapman's of 1923. The exception is Kathryn Sutherland's 1996 re-editing for Penguin Classics, which, in conformity with the policy of that series, returns to the first edition as the base text.[20] I doubt whether I would have found the punctuation of *Mansfield Park* so interesting without Professor Sutherland's work. She highlights the way that the lighter, more cursory punctuation of 1814 reflects the inflections of language as actually spoken and heard. In her edition and a supporting article, she has challenged the orthodoxy that has grown up around this text by arguing that this 'acoustic trace' takes us closer to the novel as Austen conceived it. The idiosyncratic earlier punctuation of the 1814 text reflects 'heard, (as opposed to seen and read) conversational and counter-grammatical rhythms',[21] she suggests. Furthermore, '[t]here is a "freshness and freedom about *MP* (1814) which is lost in the regularizations and corrections" begun in *MP* (1816) and continued by Chapman'.[22] The text with which we are familiar, then, in Chapman and other editions, is the joint production of Austen, her compositors, her publishers and her editors. This is analogous, perhaps, to the varnishing and framing of an artist's canvas and the hanging of it in a public gallery: it represents, to a degree that may damage the author's original conception, the co-option and institutionalising of the original work.

Sutherland's arguments are persuasive—and they will have an influence on all subsequent editors of this, and perhaps many other, texts. The earlier text, closer to the author's own manuscript version, does reflect a system of punctuation more closely bound to speech. Moreover, one can certainly configure the relation in gender terms—as the imposition of males, standard bearers of the grammatical Law, onto a (presumed defective) female original. But I am not at all sure at this point whether it follows that the first edition therefore should be the base text of an edition of this novel. This depends on a premise—avowedly a Romantic premise—that the original 'utterance' has an authenticity that later revisions (even if they are by the author) lack. But Austen was not a Romantic author, certainly even less a Romantic than Scott: and it seems to me an integral part of the 'story' of *Mansfield Park* that it was taken up by the Tory establishment—for that is what publication and publicity by Murray effectively means. Moreover, one can argue, Austen invited, indeed welcomed, this establishment's embrace. Quite apart from the technical aspect (as I have shown here, some of the changes made for the second edition are improvements likely to have been made by Austen herself) perhaps as a matter of principle an edition ought to reflect and embody such a history.

Certainly, then, the Cambridge edition, in choosing the second edition of *Mansfield Park* as its base text, will be endorsing and continuing the novel's career as a 'classic' as well as describing and commenting upon that career. What we are looking at, as Sutherland has herself suggested, is the process by which a text by an unknown female author is adopted into the mainstream, brought into the possible pantheon (one feature of Murray's correspondence is the constant preoccupation with the 'immortality' of his authors' works). As a result of a downturn in publishing, John Murray sold his copyrights in the novels, and the next appearance of *Mansfield Park* was in Bentley's series of Standard Novels in 1833. Soon after, in 1842, the copyright expired. The 'Standard Novels' were not all to make it into the canon—but this was the decisive next step in *Mansfield Park*'s dissemination and elevation.

7

(De)colonising *Mansfield Park*

Mansfield Park, as everyone knows, is Jane Austen's imperialist novel. This is not because *Mansfield Park* is Austen's imperialist novel, but because the topic has been so much talked up in the last twenty years, and because the film of the same name, released in 1998, brought this interpretation to a wider audience. Its currency is mainly due to Edward W. Said's section, 'Jane Austen and Empire' in his *Culture and Imperialism* (1993) but the engine was running for at least ten years before that.[1] Once the notion that slavery in Antigua, in Susan Fraiman's striking phrase, is 'the dark underbelly of *Mansfield Park*'[2] caught hold, it rapidly became standard, endlessly repeated as a key to this otherwise famously 'difficult' text. The two recent North American editions of the novel for instance give this reading prominence: three of the nine articles presented for students' instruction in the Norton, edited by Claudia L. Johnson, are on the topic of slavery.[3] A recent commentator sums up the scene accurately enough: '*Mansfield Park* used to be viewed as Jane Austen's most quietist, ahistorical work', writes Kate Trumpener, but is 'now often re-read as a novel engaged with the events of its day—the abolition of the slave trade, the French revolution, political upheaval in the Caribbean'.[4] It is perhaps not too much to say that postcolonial criticism now has a controlling interest in, if not possession of, this text. It has colonised *Mansfield Park*.

The Miramax film called *Mansfield Park* written and directed by Patricia Rozema displays this colonisation in its most ruthless form.[5] Opening with a slave ship moored off the English coast, Rozema's script dramatises that intertwining of the Bertram family's fortunes with their estate in Antigua and slavery that postcolonial criticism has reiterated. Its Sir Thomas, played very effectively by Harold Pinter as a heavy-jowelled patriarch of thunderous presence, is an incarnation of feminist and postcolonial critical portrayals of him as a proto-Gothic tyrant. The film sees parallels everywhere between the position of the young women at Mansfield and the position of the slaves on the Bertram estates, and in this too reproduces and transmits the claims of recent criticism. *Mansfield Park*, wrote Joseph Lew for instance, in 1991, using a phrase of Thomas Clarkson, 'dramatizes . . . "the Slavery and Commerce of the Human Species"'.[6] June Sturrock writes in her Introduction to the recent Broadview edition of the novel that 'Sir Thomas, the slave-owner, seeks absolute rule over the women of his family. He regards them as his property, subject to his will and disposable for profit, like his slaves,'[7] reiterating Peter Smith's earlier claim that '[i]t is Fanny who is the slave'.[8] Susan Fraiman writes of 'Sir Thomas's bid . . . to put female flesh on the auction block in return for male status',[9] a motif faithfully replicated in Rozema's staging of Sir Thomas's handling of Fanny in the marriage market. At the film's emotional climax, she finds Tom's plantation sketchbook with its Goyaesque depictions of a Sir Thomas engaged in various forms of cruelty and sexual perversion with slaves. In the words of a fifth critic, Moira Ferguson, he 'represents men who control the general slave population and the female slave in particular through varieties of abuse'.[10]

Sir Thomas is a key figure in postcolonial readings of the novel, though the critical issues are far broader than this.[11] Trevor Lloyd has shown convincingly, however, that Said's assertion that 'the Bertrams would not have been possible without the slave trade, sugar and the colonial planter class' is unlikely to be tenable.[12] Through an examination of details of the Bertram finances actually recorded in the novel, and drawing on John Habakkuk's *Marriage, Debt and the Estates System,*

English Landownership 1650–1950, (1994) he demonstrates how small a portion of the family's income is likely to have come from the trade in sugar. Much of the information about the estate's finances drawn on by other critics comes from the mouth of Mrs Norris—and how reliable is she about money matters? It is certainly clear that Austen emphasizes that the Northamptonshire estate is a prosperous, income-generating enterprise, and nothing suggests that Antigua 'sustains', as Said put it, the family's income. If Lloyd is right, one of the premises on which postcolonial interpretation of this novel is founded falls to the ground. My purpose in this chapter is to dispute some of the other premises of the postcolonial approach, to examine the critical strategies by which matters marginal to the novel have been moved to its centre, and indicate the political ends this serves. Moreover, the 'myth', as Lloyd calls it, of the Antiguan connection, once cleared away, like varnish scraped from a painting, may enable us to see some features of this text more clearly.

Mansfield Park is certainly the most referential of Austen's novels, a 'condition of England' narrative before the phrase was invented. All three of the books written and probably conceived after Austen settled down to write at Chawton after 1809 mark a break from the ethos of *Pride and Prejudice*, published in 1813, only a year before *Mansfield Park*'s appearance. *Pride and Prejudice* (comparatively speaking) is set in an eighteenth-century Never-Never land. Places are entirely fictional, dating is vague, and dreams come true. By contrast *Mansfield Park*, which begins '[A]bout thirty years ago', is precisely set in the years after the abolition of slavery in 1807, and very possibly at the same time as its composition.[13] It contains extended discussions of current topics such as the 'improvement' of estates (including mentions of a 'Mr Repton', still alive at the time of publication), the role of the clergy and the Established Church in contemporary society, and the system of 'interest' which determines, for instance, whether young William Price gets on in his career or not. Behind the domestic life of the novel a wider geographical and historical scene is implied—whether it is Sir Thomas Bertram's absence abroad which allows his children to make free of the house and rehearse the recent hit play *Lovers' Vows*, or the embarkation of a ship to join the campaign against Napoleon which spoils Fanny Price's reception at her home in the important naval base of Portsmouth.

A key reference in postcolonial criticism is the name of the estate itself. 'The title of *Mansfield Park* is allusive and ironic', wrote Margaret Kirkham in her pioneering book *Jane Austen, Feminism and Fiction* of 1983,[14] calling attention to the judgment of Lord Mansfield, given in 1772, that slavery was illegal on English soil. This contention is the seed of the currently dominant assumption that Sir Thomas Bertram is first and foremost to be identified as a slave-owner. The judgment is casually mentioned by Johnson in a letter to Boswell of 1776, which Jane Austen might have read in Boswell's *Life*.[15] In fact, Mansfield gave it as his opinion that since slavery was so 'odious' a condition, 'nothing can be suffered to support it, but positive law'. His judgment was given 'with evident reluctance' and he spoke of the 'inconveniencies' that might follow from the decision, so it is not clear whether the reference would be to his liberalism or his prejudice. Mansfield, as a great man of the age, is mentioned many times by Boswell, and there is no reason why this, of all his judgments, is the one signalled by Austen.[16] The reference (if it is that) is ambivalent, to say the least. Perhaps there is no reference at all. 'Mansfield' could be as vaguely significant as, say, Woodhouse—both of them English placenames. The title of Murray's earldom, awarded in 1776, was taken from the town of Mansfield in Nottinghamshire. The name suggests this Scot's wish to integrate into British society, and Austen may have chosen it too for its representative Englishness. It is more likely that if there is an allusion in the name it is to a novel she knew back to front, Samuel Richardson's *Sir Charles Grandison*.[17] One of the hero's many good deeds is to introduce his widowed uncle to a Lady Mansfield: he travels to visit her and indeed stays at 'Mansfield-house', which those who get as far as the fifth volume learn is 'only a few miles away' from the wonderful Sir Charles's own home, Grandison-hall. (Austen's fictional *Mansfield Park* is in Northamptonshire—the county to which the family of *Grandison*'s heroine, the attractive Harriet Byron, belongs.) The name Mansfield then is, at the very least, overdetermined.

Another name that seems to postcolonial readers to confirm the text's preoccupation with slavery is Mrs Norris's. John Norris occurs in Thomas Clarkson's *History of the Abolition of the Slave Trade*, a book which it is a fair surmise Austen had read. Norris, as Clarkson relates, after first supporting the efforts of the abolitionists, changed sides and became an agent for the slavers of Liverpool. But Mrs Norris's name is also overdetermined. 'This false nurturer's name derives from the French "nourrice" and English "norrice"', writes Jocelyn Harris, persuasively amplifying a suggestion first made by Barbara Hardy in 1975.[18] Far from giving nourishment and fostering, Mrs Norris lives her emotional life by battening on others, especially her nieces, but also those servants who can conveniently be fussed and tyrannised over at the same time. She takes, rather than gives, sustenance—pheasant's eggs, cream cheese from Sotherton. Pleased with herself for preventing Dick Jackson, the carpenter's son, from getting a free dinner in the servants' hall, she scrounges soup to nurse a sick nursemaid. But her apparent kindness is as dubious as all her protestations of generosity and benevolence, like her concern for the old coachman's rheumatism that results in his riding over ten miles of unmade road in freezing weather. Mrs Norris's ministrations to others, indeed, take place under the sign of the vampire. Seen in this light, the name Norris is a piece of wit, not an ideological reference.

But of course the association of Mrs Norris with slavery is central to the postcolonial readings of the novel. They depend upon the transference of practises associated with the distant colonial outpost to the domestic scene of Mansfield itself. Since the references to Antigua and to slavery in the text are brief and apparently slight, it is vital that Mansfield estate itself, the real site of the action, be redescribed. Hence in Moira Ferguson's influential 1991 article '*Mansfield Park*, Slavery, Colonialism and Gender' there is no question of *Mansfield Park* being idealised, as in Said's piece: instead it is a mirror image of the slave estate, and this is a strategy followed by almost all postcolonial interpreters. 'The unceremonious removal of Fanny from Portsmouth to Mansfield constitutes a figure for the violent uprootings of the slave trade,' declares Carl Plasa, for instance.[19] Like a slave, Fanny is brought to Mansfield in order to service the needs of her supposedly benevolent sponsors, including, as Ferguson contends, the 'overseer' or agent of the master, Mrs Norris.[20] 'In *Mansfield Park* the colonization of Antigua is linked to the colonization of Fanny Price's mind and body: both are crucial to the maintenance of *Mansfield Park*', Barbara K. Seeber's recent book reiterates.[21]

The critical forging of this 'link', however, can be performed in various ways. Thus, Said writes that Austen '*synchronises* domestic with international authority', or that 'the domestic or small scale movement in space *corresponds* to the larger, more openly colonial movements of Sir Thomas'.[22] 'Power relations within the community of *Mansfield Park re-enact and refashion* plantocratic paradigms,' writes Ferguson.[23] The conceptual or logical gap between 're-enacting' and 'refashioning' is spanned by other critics through terminology that does not necessarily attribute to Austen conscious knowledge of what she was doing. Plasa, for example, writes about the novel's 'processes of doubling—the *figurative reinscription* of the colonial in the domestic'.[24] Clara Tuite, elaborating Said's '*homology*' between the marriage plot and post emancipation imperialism, writes that 'the plots of domestic retrenchment are *critically implicated within* those of colonial expansion'.[25] Moves like these, as well as more conventional terms such as 'counterpoint' and 'analogy', are crucial to the postcolonial argument: they are the means by which imperialist motifs and meaning are squeezed out of what would otherwise be merely domestic notations of the text. The concepts of 'figuration' and 'metonymy' in particular permit great latitude of interpretation; for Tuite, Mrs Norris's 'green curtain metonymizes the estate in Antigua, and the colony exploited for its natural resources behind the scenes'.[26]

The parallel between women as commodities and the position of slaves was in fact commonplace in the era of *Mansfield Park*.[27] Mary Wollstonecraft wrote, for instance, in the *Vindication of the Rights of Women*: 'Is one half of the human species, like the poor African slaves, to be subject to prejudices that brutalize them?'[28] Hannah More, from the other side of politics, issued a pamphlet in 1805 called 'The White Slave Trade, hints towards forming a bill for the Abolition of the White Female Slave Trade, in the Cities of London and Westminster,' in which she compares the entry into society of fashionable young women with the auctioning of slaves. 'A multitude of fine fresh young slaves are annually imported at the age of seventeen or eighteen: or, according to the phrase of the despot, [Society] *they come out.*'[29] Wollstonecraft agrees: 'What can be more indelicate than a girl's coming out in the fashionable world? Which, in other words, is to bring to market a marriageable miss. . . .'[30] There can be no doubt that *Mansfield Park* participates in this rhetoric. The novel announces its use of the theme or trope unequivocally in the first conversation between the sophisticated Crawfords and the Bertram brothers about just this topic of 'coming out' (*MP*, Volume I, Chapter 5, 48–51). Whether or not Miss Price is 'out' serves to place her with the Crawfords, and simultaneously to indicate the Bertrams' and Crawfords' participation in the rituals of high 'Society'. On the occasion of the ball thrown for Fanny and William, the narrator deliberately picks up this earlier theme, remarking curtly that 'Miss Price had not been brought up to the trade of *coming out*' (*MP*, Volume II, Chapter 9, 267).

It is at this point, however, that the notion of a structural equivalence between genteel women and slaves wears thin, or rather works at such a level of abstraction that it traduces the text. It is difficult to understand how a modern reader of even a few of the genuine narratives by slaves, or the diaries of their masters, could possibly think that there is any but the loosest relation between the state of slavery and the condition of a genteel young English woman as depicted in the novel. Take the Jamaican diaries of Thomas Thistlewood for example—a particularly relevant one, since this is a probable source for Rozema's depiction of Sir Thomas Bertram's West Indian activities.[31] Thistlewood, apparently well-read and seemingly not in general unkind, inflicted grotesque punishments on his slaves, repeatedly flogged and branded them, sometimes on the face, and recorded his frequent sexual usage of the females (with details as to the various positions adopted). A traveller to the Leeward Islands between 1807 and 1810, John Augustine Waller, described slaves in general as 'only a herd of the human species reduced to the most abject misery, considered, even by themselves, as an inferior order of beings in the scale of creation'.[32] Marriage—so crucial to the novel—was unknown among slaves.

Pursuing this supposed analogy or parallel, however, enables postcolonial readers to see the adoption of Fanny as a purely commercial event. Sir Thomas then treats her and his daughters as property, to be married off for economic and political advantage. 'Having accustomed himself to exerting de facto absolute power over his Negro chattel . . . Sir Thomas expects an identical submission from the inhabitants of Mansfield, females especially,'[33] writes Lew. Such linkages elide crucial distinctions. It would undoubtedly be convenient for Sir Thomas Bertram if his daughter married Mr Rushworth, also a member of Parliament of the same 'interest'. He allows this to override his instinctive feeling that Maria does not love her intended fiancé and ought not to marry him. But Maria, who has her sights set on a house in town, is not simply a chattel, or a vehicle of her father's political ambitions, and in allowing her father to believe what is most convenient for him to believe, she has designs of her own.[34] Even Fanny, who nostalgically longs for the 'elegance, propriety, regularity, harmony' of *Mansfield Park* (*MP*, Volume III, Chapter 13, 391) profits daily from the family's estate and social position. These young women are beneficiaries of a system in which slaves partially generated the wealth and comfort they enjoy.[35] They are lesser beneficiaries than the males, but the key issue of consent (which the novel of course foregrounds) means that they are free as no slave, by definition, is. More and Wollstonecraft were good publicists and knew the value of enlisting the liberal sentiment that had been aroused by the abolition agitation to bolster their own causes. But in itself the comparison has little more purchase than the commonplace notion of 'slaving'—'I have been slaving myself till I can hardly stand' (166)—which Austen puts into the mouth of the canting Mrs Norris. By erasing the difference between genteel young women at the centre and a subjugated race at the periphery, this apparently radical criticism merely reiterates a familiar conservative anglo-centric gesture.[36]

As I've said, this interpretation of the novel depends upon an analogy between Mansfield and the estate in Antigua. Mrs Norris says that the estate is making 'poor returns' and Sir Thomas's presence is necessary to put things to rights, but little else is said about it. Obviously the more we can construe about the situation there, the more we can say about the events and characters that the text does concentrate on. Postcolonial criticism thus works energetically to fill that gap. Joseph Lew, for example, taking it for granted that Sir Thomas is a member of the West Indian lobby in Parliament, tries hard, by linking the figure to 'contemporary stereotypes of white West Indian society', and by citing Mathew Lewis's 1845 *Journal of a Residence among the Negroes in the West Indies,* to suggest 'what Sir Thomas Bertram may have experienced on arriving at his Antigua estates'.[37] 'How many slave concubines has Sir Thomas Bertram? 'Given certain much-touted facts about planters', Moira Ferguson writes, 'contemporaries could have amplified Sir Thomas's character. . . . Planters were infamous for taking slave mistresses and fathering children.'[38] Ferguson claims, too, that 'he is fictionally characterised as one of those members of parliament who defended plantocratic interests', and this is amplified by other critics, notably by Brian Southam, who writes that Sir Thomas, 'one of the West Indian lobby', 'would have voted for the trade's continuation over the twenty years that Abolition was contested at Westminster'.[39]

Mansfield Park says nothing about Sir Thomas's parliamentary activities.[40] An interesting comparison is to be found in Mary Brunton's *Discipline*, published a year after *Mansfield Park*. There, the hero Maitland is '[h]imself a West India merchant, and interested, of course, in the continuation of the slave trade'. Nevertheless the novelist seems to believe it plausible that 'he opposed, with all the zeal of honour and humanity, this vilest traffic that ever degraded the name and character of man. In the senate of his country he lifted up his testimony against this foul blot upon her fame. . . .'[41] Because Sir Thomas has estates in Antigua it does not follow that he is for the slave trade. It is not at all likely, as Lloyd argues, that Sir Thomas, a provincial Member whose West Indian estate makes up a minor share of his income, would form part of the West Indian or planter 'interest'. The fact that he is so pleased about the prospective connection with Rushworth—'in the same county and the same interest'—is evidence on the contrary that he identifies himself firmly with the English landowning class. The point, of course, is not whether Sir Thomas was or was not: it is the degree to which postcolonial criticism, driven by ideological imperatives, allows itself imaginative extrapolation of the text.

It is possible, rather, that Austen specifically chose Antigua as the place from which the Bertram family drew a large part of their income not only because this compromises the family, but in order to frustrate simple moral indignation. Austen's readers would certainly have understood that the family were one of the very large section of the British gentry who drew part of their income from a West Indian estate. Ruth Perry notes the efforts of Captain Wentworth in the last page of *Persuasion* (251) to put Mrs Smith 'in the way of recovering her husband's property in the West Indies', which are the occasion of the text's commendation, without a whisper as to the dubiousness of an income thereby obtained.[42] It is at least possible, then, that Austen relied upon her readers' assumption that an income from the West Indies would be a normal, or unremarkable, part of a gentleman's estate (thus, as Said concluded, consolidating the imperial vision). As Tom Gibbon pointed out in 1982, the Rev. George Austen himself was a trustee of an estate on Antigua, held by James Langford Nibbs.[43] 'We do not call Bermuda or Bahama, you know, the West Indies', Mrs Croft remarks in *Persuasion*: her creator would not have been less precise (*P* 70.) It is probable then that Austen had definite intentions in making Sir Thomas Bertram travel not to Bermuda, Jamaica, or St Kitts, or any other of the Leeward islands but to his Antiguan estates.

Jane Austen remarks on her 'love' of Thomas Clarkson in a letter to Cassandra in the months that *Mansfield Park* was being finished.[44] She will have known of her own family's connections with Antigua,[45] and possible that she would have read the mentions of Antigua in Clarkson's *History of the Abolition of the African Slave Trade* of 1808 with particular attention. One occurs in a passage about the moral degradation of slaves, and is part of the abolitionists' Evangelical argument that eliminating the traffic would force planters to treat their slaves more kindly, and lead to the inculcation of religious principle. Wilberforce, speaking on the motion to abolish the slave trade in May 1791, declared that 'the state of degradation, to which [slaves] were reduced . . . produced an utter inattention' to slaves as 'moral agents':

They were kept at work under the whip like cattle. They were left totally ignorant of morality and religion. There was no regular marriage among them. Hence promiscuous intercourse, early prostitution, and excessive drinking, were material causes of their decrease. With respect to the instruction of the slaves in the principles of religion, the happiest effects had resulted, particularly in Antigua, where, under the Moravians and Methodists, they had so far profited, that the planters themselves confessed their value, as property, had been raised one-third by their increased habits of regularity and industry.[46]

Thus what Wilberforce is claiming here is that Antigua is an exception. There, under the influence of religious principle, slaves are 'moral agents'. The fundamental argument however here is not a moral but an economic one: good treatment pays off in 'natural increase'. Yet it is germane to the abolitionist's long-term strategy—abolition would lead to better treatment, and better treatment would ultimately qualify slaves for emancipation. In the final debate of the campaign in 1806, Lord Holland, a planter himself (but an abolitionist), reiterated that Antigua had been able to export rather than import slaves, seemingly underlining a generally understood view that this island modelled the ameliorated future for slaves that should follow abolition.[47] If Austen chose Antigua as Sir Thomas's destination with care, she might then be suggesting that, though slavery was an iniquity, Antigua represented the best that could be said for it. And although it seems strange to us, it was perfectly possible to believe, as Bryan Edwards wrote in his *History, Civil and Commercial, of the British Colonies in the West Indies* in 1801, that 'nothing is more certain than that the Slave Trade may be very wicked, and the planters in general very innocent'.[48] *Mansfield Park* may then not conceive of Sir Thomas as a corrupt, abusive planter, but rather as a gentleman who believes himself to live by high moral principles, but whose 'benevolence' is continually compromised, negated, by the economic and gender realities of the world in which he lives, and which gives him his position and power. Austen sends him to the one island on which a Christian gentleman might own estates with less compromise to his religious principles. In other words, Antigua is chosen because it contributes to that contestation of straightforward moral judgment that is present almost throughout this text.

As Brian Southam's title 'The Silence of the Bertrams' suggests, postcolonial readings are tantalized by the one moment in the novel in which slavery is mentioned—tantalized because it is touched on, only to be withdrawn from sight. Fanny Price asks her uncle about 'the slave trade', but her question is succeeded by 'dead silence'. This mention of 'the slave trade' is the origin of the postcolonial conviction that Austen's knowledge of slavery, complicit or not, conscious or not, must be dispersed throughout the rest of the text, where the 'unspeakable', or repressed, emerges in analogous or disguised forms. The challenge for the postcolonial project then, has been to fill that silence, to make that silence speak political meaning. In the final section of this essay, I propose instead that this silence bespeaks Austen's art.

Gideon Polya has invented the term 'Austenisation' to define the abolition of reference to historical atrocities that he finds in the historical record of British colonialism—specifically the 'holocaust' inflicted by the British in the Indian state of Bengal in 1769–70.[49] Polya calls this Austenisation since he adopts the view that Austen's novels exclude reference to ugly realities; in his opinion, the black hole of British history should refer not to the infamous event in Bengal of 1756 but to the occlusion of surrounding atrocities from the British historical record. One does not have to agree to find Austenisation a useful addition to the critical vocabulary. It points to Austen's characteristic technique of deploying the historical events bearing upon her narrative in such a way that the reader is simultaneously both cognisant of them, and focused on local, intimate detail. A way of putting this is to compare the way Rembrandt controls the viewer's attention to his canvas. Rembrandt paints some things with great vividness and detail, with thick and lustrous pigment: other areas in the painting— sometimes contiguous with vividly rendered parts—are merely sketched, indicated, patches of opaque paint.[50] One can catch this specific process of Austenisation at work, for instance, in the passage in which William Price is holding the assembled family enthralled by his adventures at sea whilst Mrs Norris fidgets about looking for 'two needlefulls of thread or a second-hand shirt button' (*MP*, Volume II, Chapter 6, 236). Price had, the narrator says, 'known every variety of danger, which sea and war together could offer', but these adventures—the content of his stories—are left unspecified. The passage actively guides the reader towards a different focus—Mrs Norris's mad thrift in the midst of the Bertram plenty. William's heroic narrative of 'horrors' is like the pictorial artist's 'negative shape': significant because of that which surrounds it and is painted or touched in, the actual recipient of the artist's attention and skill. In passages like this, one can watch how Austen acknowledges 'abroad', and implicitly the dependency of English domestic life upon the activities of its external agents, whilst directing her reader's attention elsewhere. And, as in *Persuasion*, this is done in the very act of exhibiting her characters' comic insularity.[51]

This mode of dealing with the grand narrative that is historically contiguous with the domestic focus of *Mansfield Park* is elaborated in the passage that is crucial to the postcolonialist reading of the text. Fanny is being encouraged by Edmund to put herself forward more:

'. . . You are one of those who are too silent in the evening circle.'

'But I do talk to him more than I used. I am sure I do. Did not you hear me ask him about the slave trade last night?'

'I did—and was in hopes the question would be followed up by others. It would have pleased your uncle to be inquired of farther.'

'And I longed to do it—but there was such a dead silence! And while my cousins were sitting by without speaking a word, or seeming at all interested in the subject, I did not like—I thought it would appear as if I wanted to set myself off at their expense, by shewing a curiosity and pleasure in his information which he must wish his own daughters to feel.'

'Miss Crawford was very right in what she said of you the other day—that you seemed almost as fearful of notice and praise as other women were of neglect. We were talking of you at the Parsonage and those were her words. She has great discernment . . .' (*MP*, Volume II, Chapter 3, 198).

Compared to this interplay between youthful cousins the reference to the slave trade is certainly, as Said put it, 'un-inflected, unreflective'—an incidental conversational topic, plausibly relevant to the period in which the novel is set, but in the background, the shadow. Behind Fanny and Edmund's conversation, in the middle distance of 'last night' is the scene in the drawing room after dinner: within this, so distant it is a mere notation, is Sir Thomas's speech; beyond that, what his speech recounts, what history it tells, is darkness. The effect of these recessive planes, analogous perhaps to Rembrandt's carefully calibrated sequences of tones, is to make the foreground seem astonishingly present—the kind of effect that Virginia Woolf, who conjured up a similar scene between the cousins, thought might show Austen 'in the act of greatness'.[52] The interplay between Edmund and Fanny here—Fanny's insecurity, Edmund's infatuation with Mary—that is what solicits the reader's attention, left to imagine what Fanny feels when she hears that Edmund and Mary have talked her over.

Moreover, the reader's attention is additionally arrested (and distracted) because the content of Fanny's supposedly shy speech about her cousins, if looked into carefully, suggests an insight into her inner life radically at odds with both Edmund's praise and the view that is assumed by the narrative's solicitation of sympathy. Fanny has assessed her cousins' deficiency as daughters with a sharp, unforgiving, envious eye. How does the reader reconcile these competing signals, this surfeit of signification? This passage, like so many others, leads then not into slavery, *per se*, but into that deeper problematic of

Mansfield Park of which the business on the Antiguan estates and how to weigh it, is just one facet. This text certainly provides information by what it hints at, reserves, denies, devolves by implication, as well as what it presents: the problem is how one juggles the various and varying assessments to which this concatenation of differing knowledges gives rise. In the foreground is the depiction of this awkward, troubled, highly intelligent young woman, stymied by her own insecurities.

Nevertheless the 'dead silence' that Fanny reports follows Sir Thomas's reply does have significance. As Clara Tuite notes, 'this moment is not a silence in or on the part of the text but a pointed representation of silence'. She immediately goes on, however, to describe it as '—Sir Thomas's silence on the subject of slavery', thus obeying the postcolonial imperative, and in effect filling in the silence.[53] But the silence cannot be a silence on the subject of 'slavery'; Fanny's question was specifically about 'the slave trade'; and the text specifically mentions 'my cousins' as the 'silent' audience who do not ask further questions of their father. Perhaps Tuite is remembering Brian Southam, who suggests that Sir Thomas's 'loquacity may have dried up at the mention of slaves', a speculation without grounds. Southam, who generally emphasizes, correctly, that the question is about the trade, abolished in 1807, later writes that 'Fanny gets no reply to her forbidden question, because none is possible from a man who has supported the slave trade.'[54] Sir Thomas does reply. Fanny's question is not 'forbidden': Edmund in fact encourages her to ask more, and says his father would have welcomed it. There is no evidence that her uncle has supported the slave trade. The silence is about his daughters, whose philistine indifference to geography and history has been well-established since their schooldays.

What do these obvious misreadings point to? This is a taxing moment for the postcolonial critic, because it is the only place in the novel in which their subject becomes explicit. Yet it is a resistant moment, and says nothing to the purpose. So burning an ideological commitment and moral passion, though, sees what it wants to see. Sir Thomas is remade into a monster—in Southam's case as a 'buyer of slaves—lawfully in times past, or even illegally since 1808'—and Fanny and Maria turned into veritable slaves themselves. What from the postcolonial perspective are gaps in the text—the veritable absence of information about Antigua, for instance—must be filled with imaginative speculation, and this speculative material must be then imposed upon (read 'linked to') the domestic life of the novel, so as to force interpretations that, depending on the critic's point of view, either reveal Austen as complicit with the imperialist project, or as skilfully exposing the complicity of her culture. Or if it does not speak what *must* be there, it is camouflaging or disguising, in Plasa's phrase, 'effaced colonial realities'.[55] For Moira Ferguson, to give a final example, the phrase 'dead silence', 'ironically speaks important debarred and smothered voices'. '"Dead silence" affirms Sir Thomas' seeming pretence that power relations are stable in Antigua. For what other than dissimulation of some sort—most likely an obfuscation or omission—could explain Fanny Price's acceptance of his lengthy speech on the slave trade. "Dead" and "silence" in other words, forswear the reality of ubiquitous slave insurrections.'[56] Fanny clearly explains why she does not follow up her question. Ferguson's account implies that Austen describes the listening family's silence in order to alert the reader's attention to the fact that her novel says nothing about slavery and slaves. But if it says nothing, it says nothing about death, or dissent, or power relations or slave insurrections.

The issue that I am dealing with here has been focused by Kathryn Sutherland, who writes that Fanny Price, 'a carefully chartered interiorised space',

has come to be seen by the late twentieth-century reader as the highly charged psychic arena which is the private 'other' of history. In readings which repoliticize what the novel's constraining domestic strategies so deliberately depoliticize, the wider significance of *Mansfield Park* as a study of family in crisis at a particular historical moment becomes more evident.[57]

The postcolonial critic, 're-politicizing' what Austen's art 'depoliticizes', is not performing an action that is merely innocent, supplementing the novel with the historical referents that it merely gestures towards or keeps hidden. Instead, it is actively colonising the novel for a movement that places more value on the 'history' that the text is putatively embedded within, than the artefact of the novel itself.

The fantasy Austen offered North American readers at the end of the nineteenth century, Mary Favret argues, is a world without the problem of race.[58] Austen becomes the site at which a civil and homogeneous world of the middle class can be imagined, precisely because in her novels the racial question is 'bleached and sanitized'. Criticism at the end of the twentieth century, I will finally suggest, demonstrates the operation of an analogous but recuperative dream. Austen knew about slavery in the West Indies but it did not preoccupy her, nor was it referred to in anything but the most marginal way in her novels: it simply represented a fact in the background of English life. The demand that slavery—or rather race relations—play a major role in the novels, or in the way the novels are read, is an articulation of contemporary political need. This is analogous to the familiar mode in which imperial culture, secure in its superiority, ignores or perverts the cultural life of indigenous peoples, 'rewriting' or construing texts to its own agenda. To put this another way, the Austen text has now become subjugated knowledge.

My argument is not merely that postcolonial criticism's attempts to make the silence speak, to fill the black hole, are acts of cultural imperialism, projecting onto the text the demands of its own ideological imperatives. Nor is it to deny that Sir Thomas's position as West Indian proprietor is without significance. What I suggest instead, is that the novel seeks almost everywhere to frustrate and complicate simple straightforward moral (or political) judgment. It is true enough to say that the novel, 'offers a leading example of the strategy of the domestic novel in recasting political relations as domestic relations',[59] but this praise, characteristically, refuses to acknowledge what 'strategy' really entails. As Perry puts it, 'Austen's relation to colonialism and slavery is . . . neither more or less than one might have predicted from her gender and class.'[60] On the other hand, the novel is full of narrative innovations and dexterities that are of the essence of Austen's artistic achievement: this is Austenisation, the definitive act of genius. In effect, the postcolonial readings of the novel pass over the text's own complexities in order to propagate a simple, correct, version of their own. Jane Austen's *Mansfield Park* is thus a 'testament betrayed' in Milan Kundera's resonant phrase.[61] A work of art that (until its final chapters) suspends and impedes our routine judgments is flattened into orthodoxy to suit ordinary mortals like ourselves.

8

The Comedy of *Emma*

One of the best ways to begin a course on Jane Austen's novels, or to introduce *Emma*, is to set Austen's work within the context of contemporary female authors, as she indeed invites her readers to do in the fifth chapter of *Northanger Abbey*. The most commonly taught, and the most useful of these is Frances Burney and the novel usually chosen is her first, *Evelina*—for the good reason that young readers still find it enjoyable. Another is that Burney is the novelist whose works are most frequently alluded to in Austen's; she seems to have remained a life-long favourite, since there are references to *Cecilia* in *Persuasion* and to *Camilla* in the late, unfinished *Sanditon*.

The general relevance of Burney's first novel to Austen is readily brought out. Its subtitle, 'The History of a Young Lady's Entrance into the World' sums up the narrative of *Northanger Abbey*. The plot of a young woman from the country, who must find her way within a more sophisticated society, negotiating its unexpected challenges and steering clear of predatory males, surviving to marry, handsomely, into the patrimony, is echoed in almost all of Austen's novels. Even more important, perhaps, was the attitude that Burney (at least intermittently) took towards her heroine. Good-hearted as she is, Evelina simultaneously makes a series of silly mistakes. The reader is encouraged to feel warmly towards this innocent and naive young woman, but at the same time to find her youthful presumptions and errors amusing. (Letter VIII, for example, shows Evelina trying to persuade herself she doesn't want to go to London, whilst every second line reveals how intensely she does.)

Recent criticism of Burney depicts a novelist who is strikingly unlike Austen. It has emphasized 'the dynamics of fear', the 'chronicle of assault', the 'trauma of growing up female', the 'fictions of violation' in *Evelina* and in Burney's later novels. Much less has been said about those aspects of the novel that endeared it to, and entertained, Burney's contemporaries: the range of its comedy from affectionate irony to satire, slapstick and burlesque, and its gallery of vividly depicted characters. For, though there are certainly in *Evelina* passages of terror (and melodrama), the frame and design of the novel is comic. And it is as a female comic novelist that Burney was probably most useful and most instructive to Austen—and is certainly most useful to the instructor who wants to describe the comedic mode of *Emma*. The would-be genteel Branghton girls, and their beaus, Mr Brown and Mr Smith (whom Dr Johnson and Mrs Thrale especially enjoyed) are obviously a template for Austen's later handling of such figures as the Steele sisters in *Sense and Sensibility*, as well as the Eltons in *Emma*. The Branghtons' vulgarity is less important than the fact that their 'ill-breeding' is aligned with 'brutality', most markedly in their treatment of their poverty-stricken lodger, the poet Mr Macartney, just as the Eltons' is with their cruel treatment of poor Harriet Smith at the ball. Not co-incidentally, 'brutality' is what Emma accuses herself of in her dealings with Miss Bates.

The lines of social class, then, underscore the comedy of *Evelina*, just as they do that of *Emma*. Primarily, however, though Burney and Austen are similarly comic novelists, the comedy of Burney's novel offers a clear and instructive *contrast* with the comedy of Jane Austen. Macaulay long ago pointed out that Burney excelled in eccentrics, whilst Austen's figures were much more delicately and subtly differentiated from each other and individualised. But this is not what is perhaps most striking when one teaches the two novelists together. For, varied as it is, the comedy of Burney's novel can be summed up as the comedy of discomfort. Laughter in Burney's novel is habitually in the enjoyment of another's discomposure—whether this be the overturning of Madame Duval's carriage, toppling her into the mud, or Mr Brown's being caught arm in arm with prostitutes, or in Mrs Selwyn's witty assaults on the vanity of Lovel and Lord Merton. When Madame Duval relates the episode of the carriage ambush to the Branghtons, expecting their sympathy, the men burst into laughter, and the young ladies, at first straight-faced, stuff their handkerchiefs into their mouths. We share their laughter whilst laughing at them for laughing. Here, as with the notorious later episode of Lovel's being attacked by a monkey dressed as a fop, the novelist is playing the scene for a derisive laughter that she simultaneously condemns (those who stand aloof, like Evelina and Lord Orville, are commended for their benevolence). The simultaneous participation in a character's amusement, and comic irony towards it is found also in *Emma*, though to quite different effect.

Apart from this kind of crude comedy, social discomfort is the motif of all the amusement to be had from the Branghtons' misunderstanding of genteel arrangements, as it is from Evelina's own slips, mistakes and social embarrassments. The comedy of *Emma*, the kind of response elicited by the comedy of *Emma*, is quite different. A tiny incident, embedded deep in the text, could usefully serve a teacher to bring out the salient characteristics of Austen's quite distinct comic sense. This is the moment when Miss Bates confides to Jane in the midst of a long speech, itself in the midst of the ball at the Crown, that Mrs Bates has been a bit disappointed at her outing to Mr Woodhouse's because, having been offered 'a delicate fricassee' of sweetbread and asparagus, the treat has been withdrawn on Mr Woodhouse's fearing that the asparagus is a trifle underdone (329). We are amused at both these old people: at Mrs Bates's expectation of a delicacy (perhaps we imagine the look on her face as the dish is sent away) and at Mr Woodhouse's fussiness here, once again carried to an absurd extreme. And we are both amused and dismayed at the frustration of Emma's kindly endeavours to provide care for their guest. But we do not, I think, mock either of the figures involved, nor Emma or Miss Bates.

This tiny episode might suggest to a class the comic form of *Emma* in embryo. This is not the comedy of discomfort, but of mutual good intentions gone awry: the comedy of comfort, perhaps. It is a miniature comedy of cross-purposes. We enjoy this little moment the more because it forms an item in the running joke about food at Hartfield. Mr Woodhouse's little executive action is a successful move in that submerged domestic battle that began in the novel with Emma's own successful sabotage of her father's wishes about Miss Weston's wedding cake at the end of Chapter 2. Every time dietary preferences are in question at Hartfield this comic motif is repeated (and with it, the novel's acknowledgment of the claims of the body, the corporeal.) In fact, a comedy of cross-purposes often gathers round the figure of Mr Woodhouse. It is there for example in those scenes in which he and his daughter Isabella comfortably converse together, but are always in danger of veering off the broad road of their apparent mutual obsession with health and illness and crashing into each other. The reader watches with growing amusement each time Isabella bring up her doctor Mr Wickfield's advice and Mr Woodhouse brings up his doctor Mr Perry's, knowing that sooner or later, and despite Emma's efforts to take the reins, they will charge into each other. It is interesting that Jane Austen was pleased by Scott's especial commendation of these two characters in his early review of the novel.

The comedy of cross-purposes necessarily involves two or more participants, and sets the amused reader apart from both. Since it inheres in the total situation, it is not often a cruel comedy, enjoying a figure's bodily indignity (Madame Duval in the mud; Sancho Panza being tossed in the blanket) but one that savours, ruefully, the spectacle of human misunderstanding wrought to its acutest pitch. For this comedy to yield its greatest delight, the participants must not just misunderstand, they must each interpret *the very same thing* in a different fashion, attribute to the same sign contradictory meaning. Such a comedy depends, too, upon the creation of individuals as agents, as figures with definable intentions and schemes, thus of an Emma rather than an Evelina. In the first volume of *Emma*, Emma's plot to marry Harriet to Mr Elton is productive of much comedy of this kind. Emma sees the portrait as signifying 'Harriet is a very pretty girl' and Mr Elton's praise of it as overtures of courtship. For Mr Elton, on the other hand, the portrait signifies Emma's genteel accomplishments, and his flattery is meant to further his courtship of her. Once given the hint, a class on the novel will be able to find many other examples of comic cross-purposes in these chapters, for here they reach a near-farcical pitch. They come to a head in that scene in the carriage where Mr Elton, turned by 'Mr Weston's good wine' into a hometown impersonation of Sir Clement Willoughby leaping into the carriage with Evelina and 'actually' grasping her hand in his (108) is found 'actually making violent love' (129) to Emma. The adverb catches, as in Burney, not only the immediacy of the scene, but Emma's astonishment, and—to the reader, who has seen what is coming, her comical—indignation.

The comedy of *Emma*, then, is the comedy of cross-purposes. Later in the novel it is merged or cohabits with something more subtle. When Miss Bates tells Jane Fairfax about her grandmother, a little window, or vista, opens upon another mode of life. The moment is an aperture within an incursion, for Miss Bates's speech itself appears to trespass on Emma's consciousness. (Thus it might help to demonstate to students how Austen contrives that we shall feel the depth of her created world.) Mrs Elton and Mrs Weston, we gather, have vied for the privilege of offering their carriage to bring Miss Bates and Jane to the ball, and Miss Bates is full of gratitude: 'Never were such neighbours' she enthuses (322). But in this second long speech, again overheard unwillingly by Emma, we learn that this woman, for whom a shabby village inn decorated and lit by candles has become a 'fairyland', has had to slip out, in the midst of the festivities, to 'run home' to put her elderly mother to bed. No-one has offered their carriage for this errand, and as she says, 'nobody missed me'. Thus, quite unknown to Emma, the realities of class in this community are inscribed: Miss Bates' considerate dutifulness differs remarkably from the forms of charity that are extended to her. And this is nested in a speech which we are invited to find, and do find, in its garrulous inconsequence, amusing.

Miss Bates's chatter here exemplifies a variation on the notion of cross-purposes—what we might call, pushing it a little further, comic self-contradiction. It is a variety of the kind of speech that Austen often uses to expose her characters, in which, for example, Mrs Bennet complains 'that those who never complain are never pitied', or Mrs Norris boasts of her charitable nature in sentences which reveal just how mean-minded she is. Mr Weston tells Emma that he never allows himself 'to speak ill' of Mrs Churchill on his son's account, but this doesn't prevent him from ending his confidences with 'she has no more heart than a stone to people in general; and the devil of a temper' (121). Miss Bates first protests that she doesn't want to pre-empt Jane's telling her grandmother with whom she danced, and then does, and soon protests that she doesn't want the disappointment over the sweetbread and asparagus to reach Miss Woodhouse's ears, at the same time as she is broadcasting it all over the room. Wrapping round it, of course, is yet another form of amusement for the reader: for if Emma were able really to attend to what Miss Bates is saying she would certainly understand the world she lives in rather better, and she might even remark Frank Churchill's attentions to Jane.

The comedy of cross-purposes reaches its apotheosis in the scene of Mr Knightley's proposal. The cross-purposes of farce have been kept up—perhaps stretched too far?—in the mix-up between Frank Churchill's chivalrous rescue of Harriet from the gypsies, and Mr Knightley's chivalrous rescue of her from the Eltons. Now Emma believes that Harriet might be right about Mr Knightley's feelings for her, and dreads to hear the news. Walking in the garden at Hartfield, each is apprehensive about the other's emotional investments, and each fears that the other is in love with someone else. They are matched in their equal misunderstanding. Emma interprets Mr Knightley's demeanour as a signal that he has encountered his brother's displeasure at the prospective match with Harriet; he interprets her hesitancy as disappointment at Frank Churchill's engagement to Jane. Thus the ground-plan of their conversation resumes the many comic misunderstandings (including those between the two of them) with which the novel has familiarised the reader. The dialogue seems to be moving towards final clarification, when Emma, thinking that Mr Knightley is on the point of telling her about Harriet, stops him: '"Don't speak it, don't speak it," she eagerly cried. . . . "Thank you," said he, in an accent of deep mortification, and not another syllable followed' (429). At this point their being at cross-purposes becomes potentially tragic.

Farcical misunderstanding requires that the same signal or sign be read in contradictory ways. Here the misunderstanding is in fact resolved through the very words that seem to take it even further. Emma, unable to let Mr Knightley suffer, offers to listen to him 'as a friend'. There is something wonderfully complementary in this gesture, since it is because he is 'satisfied with proving myself your friend', that Mr Knightley has spoken to Emma most earnestly at their most intense previous encounter at Box Hill. On that occasion Mr Knightley has put himself, his own desires and prospects, aside in order to put himself at what he believes is the other's service. Here, Emma does the same. Neither quite realises that 'as a friend' in this novel now means, if not 'as a lover', as one who truly loves. "As a friend!" repeats Mr Knightley, "that I fear is a word—". Then he sees. "Emma, I accept your offer—Extraordinary as it may seem, I accept it, and refer myself to you as a friend.— Tell me, then, have I no chance of ever succeeding?" (430) Thus the comedy of cross-purposes reaches its consummation.

Much recent criticism of Jane Austen has embedded her work within the context formed by her contemporary women novelists. We can now read her novels as dialogically engaged with those writers, Burney among them, and, as I've suggested, *Evelina* offers some useful entry-points for a class thinking about the specific achievement of *Emma*. But this feminist-historicist criticism, valuable as it is, has obscured an important aspect of Austen's literary inheritance. It has perpetuated the neglect of Austen's relation to the theatre. For it is probably even more useful to open a discussion of the novel with *The School for Scandal* or *She Stoops to Conquer*. The comedy of *Emma* is indebted to the 'laughing comedies' that succeeded sentimental comedy on the eighteenth-century stage, and to the plays that Austen herself saw and alludes to, as familiarly as our students do 'Friends' or 'Sex in the City'. Austen takes the character foibles, the over-hearings, the vanities and misunderstandings that are the staple of these plays and, reimagining them within a precisely rendered domestic setting, makes a comedy that is both subtle and moving. It could well be claimed then that Shakespeare, Garrick and Colman, Sheridan and Goldsmith provide the models for that entanglement of cross-purposes which is the dominant comic mode of *Emma*.

9

Comfort, Health and Creativity: A Reading of *Emma*

One of the chief challenges in teaching *Emma*, I've found, as with all Jane Austen's novels, is to get students to move on from talking about characters and about the romance plot and to understand something of the novel's structure and its status as a work of art. This is all the more important in the wake of the recent films, which, for very good reasons, replace Jane Austen's artistic purposes and designs by their own, and almost inevitably give a greater prominence to sexuality and romance than do the novels. In the past there have been many attempts to read *Emma* by focusing on such moral or pedagogical matters as the 'education' or 'humiliation' of Emma's imagination or (more recently) on Emma's relation to the various manifestations of patriarchal society. In this chapter I suggest an approach that picks up a relatively undernoticed preoccupation of the text, the quotidian but also salient notion of 'comfort', and seek through this to call attention to what I believe is a vital aspect of the novel's underlying conceptual, or rather emotional and ethical structure.

A way of beginning discussion of *Emma*, especially with students who have read other Austen novels, but also with those who are studying this as an example of her work for the first time, is to call attention to its densely populated textual space. One distinctive feature of *Emma* is the way it embeds its action so convincingly within a small, circumscribed, but nevertheless active and convincingly detailed 'Highbury world'. This is achieved by numerous means, but one of the most effective is the passing mention—as if they were already known to the reader—of a number of figures who never actually make an appearance in the novel. The effect of this apparently casual citation of the names of Mrs Goddard, the Coles and William Larkins, among others, is to persuade the reader that he or she already knows them, and to create a narrator who is a denizen of the world she reports so familiarly upon. One of these figures, the notice of whom serves to populate Highbury and to thicken its description is the apothecary or the local doctor.

Mr Perry is in fact mentioned in *Emma* every twenty or so pages, in one connection or other, either through Mr Woodhouse's conversation, or seen passing through the town, or through reports of his medical opinion. His presence is more than incidental to the novel, however. Of course a small town would have its local doctor, just as it would have its local school, and local shopkeepers—many of whom are named, and even briefly characterised in *Emma*—the obsequious Mrs Ford, at the draper's shop, Mrs Wallis the baker's wife, who can sometimes give a rude answer (236–7). But (one might ask) isn't Mr Perry more important, more central to the novel's main interests than these figures, as his close relation (perhaps a friendship) with Emma's father suggests? Perry, a very active figure, often glimpsed on the road, always coming back from somewhere or other, is a familiar reference for the citizens of Highbury, but he's equally important as a pointer to some of the novel's leading interests. His very activity, which is also movement up the social scale, forms a telling contrast with the genteel inertia of his principal patient in the place, Mr Woodhouse.

The threading of Mr Perry through the narrative might lead one to think about Austen's interest in health in this novel. Serious illness is rare in *Emma* (the distant Mrs Churchill's medical emergencies are treated with suspicion) and Highbury's most dramatic bodily event—Mrs Weston's pregnancy and the birth of little Anna—occurs with only the briefest of facetious mentions. But minor ailments, and imagined illnesses, coughs, colds, biliousness, fever, fainting fits, a putrid sore throat, are common occurrences in the novel, and these are matters of considerable interest to the community Jane Austen depicts. In fact one might say that talk about health is the idiolect—the characteristic mode of human exchange—in Highbury. People fuss over each other, over remedies and rhubarb, over taking cold, over draughts and diets, just as they do everywhere. *Emma* is full of the very ordinariness of such conversations and events, but whilst giving us this rich ordinariness, the novel at the same time infuses them with extraordinary narrative tension and excitement. Gossip and talk about health, highlighted extensively in the great comic dialogue in Chapter 12 in which Isabella and her father dispute the rival virtues of their favourite doctors and health resorts, is more than a source of incidental humour in the novel, one might suggest. It has a larger and more important dimension.

This is because the notion of health asks to be understood in a moral register as well as in a physical one, though the two are interconnected. The focus of this is Emma herself. The reader is introduced to Emma Woodhouse through being privy to her own consciousness, sharing her excitement at the pleasure, the game, that taking up Harriet Smith promises (23). At the same time, through the irony that the technique of free indirect discourse allows, the reader necessarily feels quite severe doubts about Emma's reasoning and motives. This mixed response to Emma's enthusiasm for Harriet is soon taken up and spelt out in the conversation between Mr Knightley and Mrs Weston in Chapter 5. One speaks of his reservations about her, the other replies by pointing out how lovely Emma is—that she is 'the complete picture of grown-up health' (39). Mrs Weston's response is superficially illogical, and doesn't meet Mr Knightley's criticisms, but at a deeper level, it does, because by speaking of Emma as 'the picture of health' Mrs Weston indicates her sense of Emma's fundamental or ontological goodness—that she is not only physically, but also emotionally and morally sound.

It's this principle of health in Emma Woodhouse that is the source of the novel's energy and warmth. For most of the book, 'spirited', capable and active, as she is, she has no difficulty in coping with the dogged timidity and resistances of her father. His ill-health (real or presumed) is also understood in a moral as well as a physical sense. He is frightened of draughts, of even short journeys in the carriage, of anything unpredictable or unforeseen or hasty. 'To have any of them sitting down out of doors to eat would inevitably make him ill', as Mr Knightley surmises (356). It would be too melodramatic, and out of harmony with the spirit of the novel, to say that he is afraid of life itself, but to put it that way suggests how the stakes in *Emma* are quite high. His invalidism is not difficult to think of as an emotional and characterological constriction or failure—and if 'eager' is one of the novel's most frequent characterising words for its heroine, by confronting that eagerness with its opposite, with invalidism and withdrawal, a profound and central ethical conflict is set up.

Another figure clearly contrasted with Emma in this respect is Jane Fairfax. 'Bless me! poor Jane is ill!' is Miss Bates's first exclamation when reading the letter that introduces her into the novel (166). This association of Jane with ill-health always shadows her, although in this instance one might share Emma's suspicion that Jane's cold is no more than a convenient pretext for her return to Highbury. But the theme of Jane's liability to illness is continued when Mr Knightley steps in to prevent her from singing herself hoarse (229) or when his brother John takes it upon himself to comment on her walking in the rain. These chivalrous interventions however are not all that they seem, for it is as if the motif of Jane's ill-health gathers together a whole set of anxieties concerned with specifically female vulnerability. Whilst Jane is thus figured as the opposite to that Emma who responds to Mrs Weston's query 'Are you well, my Emma?' with 'Oh! perfectly, I am always well, you know' (420), she is also capable of representing something about the limits and conditions of a lady's life. Jane's ill-health or the threat of it, is also a way of defining the cloud that hangs over her, the confinement of her condition, the stresses and constrictions involved in dwelling with her aunt. Miss Fairfax is pale, subject to prolonged nervous tension and anxiety, and at the climax of the novel undergoes a collapse which is clearly more emotional than physical, as Mr Perry, at this late stage of the book revealing himself as a wise and trustworthy clinician, perceives. His speech is still reported, not direct: 'Her present home, he could not but observe, was unfavourable to a nervous disorder: confined always to one room;—he could have wished it otherwise' (389). The victim of repression and anxiety, Jane is cured, as Mrs Elton archly remarks, by 'a young physician from Richmond', Frank Churchill.

In the structure of the novel Frank is homologous with Emma. His difficulties with the erratic and demanding hypochondriac Mrs Churchill are a distant reflection of hers with Mr Woodhouse. Mrs Churchill's influence acts to restrict and frustrate his erotic life in a way that parallels Mr Woodhouse's effect on Emma, though in a more material and sharper way. Like Emma, Frank is never ill. He is a figure of energy in the text, of a restless (and inevitably sexual) spiritedness that is the more frenetic, erratic, the more reckless, the more it is frustrated. His teasing, ingenuity and contrivance matches Emma's and signals to the reader that her own stratagems may well have a physical underpinning. Initially his energy is diverted into his ingenious schemes to snatch opportunities to be with Jane, partly in his amusement at hoodwinking the delightful, but to him not sexually alluring, Miss Woodhouse. His energy is expressed not only in his physical activity (he rides about the countryside a lot) but also his schemes and plans, like the ball at the Crown Inn. It's very characteristic that when, finally blocked by Jane's apparent resolution in breaking off their engagement at Box Hill, he thinks of more movement, in a wider sphere, of going abroad. His frustration communicates itself to Emma. 'The young man's spirits now rose to a pitch almost unpleasant' (374).

Frank Churchill and Mr Woodhouse meet head on over the plans for the ball at the Crown. Where the preparations for the dance are concerned Mr Woodhouse is as vocal and determined as he is anywhere in the novel. He is afraid of them all catching colds from the damp rooms inevitably found at an inn, and says so. Frank cannot resist:

'I was going to observe, Sir', said Frank Churchill, 'that one of the great recommendations of this change would be the very little danger of any body's catching cold—so much less danger at the Crown than at Randalls! Mr Perry might regret the alteration, but nobody else could.'

'Sir', said Mr Woodhouse, rather warmly, 'you are very much mistaken if you suppose Mr Perry to be that sort of character. Mr Perry is extremely concerned when any of us is ill. But I do not understand how the room at the Crown can be safer for you than your father's house.'

'From the very circumstance of its being larger, sir. We shall have no occasion to open the windows at all—not once the whole evening; and it is that dreadful habit of opening the windows, letting in cold air upon heated bodies, which (as you well know, sir) does the mischief.'

'Open the windows! But surely, Mr Churchill, nobody would think of opening the windows at Randalls. Nobody could be so imprudent! I never heard of such a thing. Dancing with open windows!—I am sure, neither your father nor Mrs Weston (poor Miss Taylor that was) would suffer it.'

'Ah Sir, but a thoughtless young person will sometimes step behind a window-curtain and throw up a sash, without its being suspected. I have often known it done myself.'

'Have you indeed sir—Bless me! I never could have supposed it. But I live out of the world and am often astonished at what I hear.' (251–2)

It is comic scenes like this that give *Emma* its distinctive quality. Ostensibly this dialogue is about physical health, but it is not hard to show that it is about much more than that. Frank's teasing is similar to, but more amiable (if more persistent) than Mr John Knightley's earlier taunting about the dangers of snow on the ground at Randalls. It's at this point that what Frank here stands for—youth, energy, enterprise—is most directly confronted with Mr Woodhouse's conservatism, once again enlisting Mr Perry, the hidden centre of the novel's circling concern with health.

Moreover at this point a key association link between health, creativity and the materially real 'open' or closed environment is suggested. Oliver Sacks has remarked that the defining condition of patienthood is 'the contraction in all realms (not least the moral realm)' and pointed conversely to 'the spaciousness of health, of full being, of the real world'.[1] This association of illness with contracture, of health with spaciousness, is translated in *Emma* into actual settings and environments. *Emma* is a novel which begins with scenes of confinement within doors that gradually diminish in frequency, as the seasons turn from winter to spring to summer, and the action bells out, the pace heats up, with occasions and expeditions. The symbolic freight or associations of indoor and outdoor settings is hinted too in such characterising declarations in the novel as 'I love an open nature', and 'Oh, if you knew how much I love everything that is decided and open!' (460). Naturally some readers, or a part of every reader, will feel that this talk about opening windows is a rather cruel and irresponsible teasing of the old gentleman, but most, I think, will recognise that our laughter is on Frank's part— that, for all his delight in mischief, he is speaking for health.

Health in *Emma* then has a spatial or material register too. In many ways, the novel suggests, health may be a more problematic matter for women than for men, for ladies than for gentlemen. Men ride about freely, to London and back in a day, or walk three miles round to pick walnuts. A lady cannot walk across the street to get letters in a light rain without attracting the kindly but interfering attention of her neighbours. The drawing room and the garden is her province. It could be said of course that Jane Austen is here merely reflecting the manners and customs of her time, but there is more to it than that. The novel connects health and energy with activity and the outdoors; indoors is associated with the stifling of energies and enterprise. The novel wants us to make a connection between confinement and ill-health (of the psychosomatic kind), and to suggest how health has some necessary connection with outgoing or openness, in all of its senses. The moments of freedom, when a woman is alone and able to walk at leisure outside, are treasured spaces in the novel: they define some of its highest points. 'Oh, Miss Woodhouse, the comfort of being sometimes alone!' Jane Fairfax exclaims when being pushed to extreme and unladylike measures she flees the strawberry party at Donwell. Here 'comfort', associated for so much of the novel with the indoors, becomes transformed into a value that overrides those conditions, paradoxically existing through solitude, freedom, exercise of free will and physical activity. 'Quick walking will refresh me,' pleads Jane (363).

This is not by any means the novel's only use of the word. Running alongside the novel's focus on health, in fact, is its attention to 'comfort'.[2] Emma's 'comfortable home' is mentioned in the very first sentence, and the word, or its cognates, recurs continually, making its unobtrusive contribution to the novel's special ambience and network of ideas. No doubt it stands for something that Jane Austen herself valued dearly. In a letter soon after she and her mother and sister had arrived at Chawton cottage in 1809, she used it in quick association with the idea of having a settled domicile at last. 'Cassandra's pen,' she writes, 'will paint our state,/ The many comforts that await/Our Chawton home. . . .'[3] All three of the novels written, or completed, at Chawton testify to the importance Austen attached to the notion of home, and to the provision of domestic comfort.[4] The word had acquired its dominant modern senses by the time Austen wrote. In earlier centuries the noun 'comfort' meant 'assistance or support' and its associated verb took the same colouring: 'Be comfortable to my mother, your mistress, and make much of her,' are Bertram's parting words to Helena in Shakespeare's *All's Well That Ends Well* (c.1602). In Johnson's *Dictionary* of 1755, comfort is still defined as meaning 'consolation, support under calamity or danger'. 'Comfort' evolved its domestic meaning in the later eighteenth century in tandem with the development of a more leisured society: it is an indisputably middle-class or bourgeois notion, depending as it usually does upon a material substrate, a steady income, for the security, placidity and ease it evolved to denote.

When we look at the dozens of references to comfort in *Emma* we find that the word is sometimes used with this material meaning uppermost, as when Mrs Weston's 'comfortable provision' is mentioned or when Mr Weston is said to have 'fitted up his house so comfortably' (13). But when Emma guiltily reflects that she has failed to add to 'the stock of the Bates's scanty comforts' (155), by not visiting them as often as she should, it is clear that the novelist employs the word to cover a far broader range of meaning. If Emma thinks sardonically about Harriet's admiration for 'the many comforts and wonders of Abbey Mill farm', she is using the word in one of its oldest senses, meaning, according to the O.E.D., 'enjoyment and delight'. Frank Churchill, in front of the Eltons' house, comments that if it were to be shared with the woman he loved, the vicarage, though small, must have ample room 'for every real comfort' (204). We hear too of Mr Woodhouse's 'comfortable talk with his dear Isabella'. Mr Perry seems to dispense comfort in this sense as well as medicines in his consultations with Mr Woodhouse (434).

'Comfort' then is clearly a concept with a wide range of suggestiveness. Whilst it points to a key value not only of the community depicted in the novel, but of the novel itself, it also rings alarm bells. Young readers will not need alerting to the idea that a world devoted to comfort, above all, is a world that has turned its back on risk, adventure, excitement. It is a seductive and problematic value. It allows no conceptual space for movement, for enterprise, for the strong, the heroic, the romantic. If one were to say that *Emma* celebrates the values of comfort one would be acquiescing in a view of Jane Austen not unlike that notoriously expressed by Charlotte Bronte.[5] Yet it is plain that the word does spring to Austen's pen when she seeks to define something important and to be treasured. In one of the novel's more remarkable references Emma thinks of it in salutation of the landscape before her at Donwell Abbey, 'It was a sweet view—sweet to the eye and to the mind.

English verdure, English culture, English comfort, seen under a sun bright, without being oppressive' (360). It is striking, once again, that Austen uses a word so much coloured by associations with the indoors to define her heroine's deepest moment of affiliation with a beloved landscape, as part of temperately phrased but none the less absolute endorsement of her communion with the qualities that landscape bodies forth. (This is three pages before Jane Fairfax is to invoke 'the comfort of being alone!') Even so, comfort is a value that might make a modern reader, so to speak, uncomfortable. It is certainly in some ways rather difficult to reconcile with that enhanced sense of health which, as I've been arguing, the novel makes pivotal to its argument.

One primary focus of comfort in *Emma* in fact is on Mr Woodhouse. 'Her father's comfort' is one of the constant preoccupations of even the Emma who with another part of her mind is busily playing imaginative games with Harriet Smith and Mr Elton and later with Jane Fairfax and Mr Dixon. 'To her he looked for comfort' (127). 'Comfort' in Mr Woodhouse's sense means only habit, familiarity, safety, a reassurance that is premised upon compensation for an unspoken or unacknowledged loss. It is a substitutive value, a consolation or solace, a secondary replacement for a failure, an emptiness, that cannot be defined. The question marks around comfort are prominent in John Knightley's unwillingness ever to leave home ('the folly of not allowing people to be comfortable at home') or when Mrs Elton pronounces platitudinously 'There is nothing like staying at home for real comfort' (274).

The problematic side of this value though emerges most sharply when Emma tells Harriet early in the novel that she will never marry since her nephews and nieces will 'supply every sort of sensation that declining life can need' and that such attachments 'suit' her 'ideas of comfort better than what is warmer and blinder' (86). At this point, it becomes especially clear that the cultivation of comfort (however broad a meaning the word may be made to carry) can be, in no very esoteric sense, self-destroying, shutting down options and denying aspects of the personality that are demonstrated in the character's vigour and decisiveness even as she speaks. Comfort also suggests a kind of dependency, something that is in strong contrast to that native energy or creative spark that is signalled so strongly when Emma is described and narratively incarnated as 'the picture of health'.

But this is far from all the novel has to say about comfort. One of the most interesting moments in which comfort is at issue in *Emma* occurs after Harriet Smith has suddenly come upon the Martins in Mrs Ford's shop. Her emotions are as confused as her grammar: 'Oh! Miss Woodhouse, I would rather done any thing than have it happen: and yet, you know, there was a sort of satisfaction in seeing him behave so pleasantly and so kindly. And Elizabeth, too, Oh! Miss Woodhouse, do talk to me and make me comfortable again.' Harriet is obviously in one sense asking to be treated as a child, 'comforted' in the sense of soothed and cossetted. But the appeal goes deeper than this, as one can see by the confusion of Emma's response. 'Very sincerely did Emma wish to do so; but it was not immediately in her power. She was obliged to stop and think. She was not thoroughly comfortable herself' (179). Emma cannot meet Harriet's demands fully, cannot respond with the unqualified acceptance of a mother, because she is herself disturbed. The encounter, as Harriet recounts it, stirs up her conscience. So though she 'exerts herself; and did try to make her comfortable, by considering all that had passed as a mere trifle, and quite unworthy of being dwelt on', this tactic is doomed to failure. Brushing both her own and Harriet's disturbance under the carpet, Emma does not address the deeper sources of Harriet's unhappiness, and so she is condemned to hear Harriet harp on the same theme for a while yet. She cannot give comfort in the deeper, more august sense that the passage also invokes. In the psychoanalyst D.W. Winnicott's phrase, she is 'not there to receive the communication': not 'there' because she is distracted by her own needs. She cannot 'hold' or 'contain' Harriet's distress and therefore cannot communicate calmness or acceptance to her friend. She cannot give a soothing that is also sustenance.

In contrast is the occasion some time later when Harriet is in a rather similar 'flutter of spirits' over Mr Elton's wedding (Volume II, Chapter 13). In this case, Emma is very clear about what she thinks, and admits her own part in Harriet's unhappiness—'Deceived myself, I did very miserably deceive you' she says with characteristic directness (268). She appeals to Harriet's love for her, and to her own pride; 'the violence of grief was comforted away', and the cure is lasting. Emma here performs the function of the good parent or mother: accepting her friend's 'unhappiness', and her own guilt, she is able to offer a kind of sustenance that arises out of her own candour and self-knowledge, a psychological 'support', that is born out of her own inner resilience and health. As these interchanges make clear, the notion of comfort moves beyond the material, and beyond compensatory and suspect 'comfort' of the sick. 'Comfort' at this point no longer has an uneasy relation to health, but seems to be a consequence of it. So we should not despise Jane Austen's attention to comfort and the comfortable in this novel.

The novel's interest in health and illness, in activity and stasis, in the indoors and the outdoors, all of which are linked and melded together, is demonstrated most moving in the staging of Emma and Mr Knightley's final reconciliation in Volume III, Chapter 13 (or 49 in modern editions). When it looks as though Harriet and Mr Knightley might marry Emma experiences her most melancholy evening, pacing about the drawing room at Hartfield, full of ominous thoughts, an evening during which her father 'could only be kept tolerably comfortable by . . . exertions which had never cost her half so much before' (422). Emma's energies are here in danger of being overtaxed, consumed by the domestic affections that whilst they are certainly part of those qualities in her that may be trusted (as Mrs Weston has put it) are in another sense the very avenues through which her young life's own project may be stemmed and frustrated. But the next day the weather clears.

With all the eagerness which such a transition gives, Emma resolved to be out of doors as soon as possible. Never had the exquisite sight, smell, sensation of nature, tranquil, warm and brilliant after a storm, been more attractive to her. She longed for the serenity they might gradually introduce; and on Mr Perry's coming in soon after dinner, with a disengaged hour to give to her father, she lost no time in hurrying into the shrubbery. (424)

The claims of comfort and health are exquisitely balanced in this climactic scene. With her father indoors, taken care of, comfortably occupied with Mr Perry, Emma is free to step outdoors, to be creative—to take those courageous and playful conversational initiatives that culminate in the clearing up of mutual misunderstandings, and lead Mr Knightley towards his declaration of love. Emma's health is thus understood, as Winnicott understood it, against a background of containing stability. Her creativity flourishes, as did Austen's as an artist, not despite, but because her 'world'—in Austen's case, cultural tradition, and family loyalty—is there in place reliably to hold and assist her. Winnicott made no bones about the significance of conception of psychological health he propounds, calling it 'the essential central element of creative originality'. There are many, many, different ways in which the greatness, the humour, the intricacy, the romance, the vigour of *Emma* can be brought out, and what I have suggested here is merely one way of configuring the novel. But there is no way round the fact that if *Emma* is an enduring masterpiece that is because it addresses issues that are at the centre of life, and of health, itself.

10

Jane Austen's England,
Jane Austen's World

All of Jane Austen's readers are familiar with those comments in her letters which compare her art to a 'little bit (two Inches wide) of Ivory' or declare that '3 or 4 families in a country village are the very thing to work on'.[1] When she writes of a 'country village', she means an *English* country village, of course, but the significance of this does not become clear until her novels are compared with those of her contemporaries. The novelists whom she praised in *Northanger Abbey*, Frances Burney and Maria Edgeworth, for instance, wrote about France and Ireland; Ann Radcliffe and Charlotte Smith, whom she also admired, wrote about Italy and America. Austen's novels are about England and English society, and deal with no other. They are never set in the south of France, the Apennines, Venice, or Switzerland; she never sends her hero or heroine to the wilds of America like Smith in *The Old Manor House* (1793) or Mary Brunton in *Discipline* (1814). She never takes them to live in Portugal and then in France, as for instance Amelia Opie does in *Adeline Mowbray* (1804).[2]

She even confines herself to England, rather than the whole of the British isles, and since this contrasts strikingly with the burlesques she wrote as an apprentice, it must have been a conscious artistic decision. As Katie Trumpener notes, 'Austen's juvenilia is strewn with journeys into Scotland and remote corners of Ireland, idyllic interludes in Welsh cottages and Scottish castles'.[3] But no Welshmen, Irish, or Jews, let alone a heroine who is the 'natural Daughter of a Scotch peer by an Italian Opera-girl' as in 'Love and Freindship' (1792) make an appearance in her mature novels. And if she never uses a European setting, she never introduces a foreigner. The domestic focus of Austen's writing has been much more emphasized, though, than her insularity, parochialism, even xenophobia.[4] Whilst Austen certainly writes of what a female poet in the *Gentleman's Magazine* of 1817 called 'woman's chiefest empire, 'Home', her carefully circumscribed English settings are all the more notable in a period in which the nationality of 'Great Britain' had been more or less consolidated.[5]

Austen is said to have loved and admired Richardson's *Sir Charles Grandison* (1756) a novel which with its intensely drawn-out conflict between the hero's passion for the Italian aristocrat Clementina, her struggle with her Catholic principles, and its many scenes set in Bologna, as well as in London and Northamptonshire, may be said to have inaugurated the 'International theme' in the British novel. Those later novelists who are often thought to be most akin to Austen, George Eliot, James and Forster, develop this international theme in their texts, not only setting portions of their narratives in foreign countries, as of course Smollett and Sterne had done before them, but going the crucial step further of playing off European culture and manners against the English. They present foreigners not merely as oddities and eccentrics, but use American, Indian and European settings, and manners, to contrast with and throw light upon the culture of the British. In this way 'Englishness' is set apart and examined, quasi-anthropologically. But there is no international theme of this kind in Jane Austen. Instead, there is a persistent thread or ground bass of English patriotism.

Austen's England then, reviewed in the historical and literary circumstances of her time, is a peculiarly confined, insulated place, cut off from the other parts of the British isles, never fully engaging with Europe. The European only appears in the novels on the peripheries, as a trace, as the absurd contaminations of language, like 'caro sposo' or the 'menus plaisirs' of a Henry Crawford, or a German play already modified to suit English taste. It is as if the real Napoleonic threat to English life and culture in her time were already diminished into the 'Bogey-man' that frightens only children, as Henry Tilney's reprimand of Catherine so strikingly enunciates. 'Remember that we are English, that we are Christians' (*NA* 197) he declares: in a 'country such as this', the terrible cannot be made novelistically plausible. When European countries are referred to, they are often generalised as the vaguely exotic 'abroad'. The empire overseas on which the prosperity and even the safety of England rests is more decisively delineated, its references more strongly inflected: but if *Mansfield Park* and *Persuasion* take care to remind the reader of these facts, they also leave geography vague and render the presence of empire in little more than its goods— the tea and coffee, Indian shawls and mahogany, out of which references the novels' realism is fabricated.

Over the past decades literary critics have stressed how much Austen's work belongs within its particular historical setting. Austen's novels certainly take part in an intertextual dialogue with other literature of the time. And certainly when one thinks about Ann Radcliffe's Italians, and Maria Edgeworth's novels of Irish rural life, and especially about the extraordinary success of Scott's *Waverley* in 1814, *Emma* (published in 1815) starts to look like a conscious effort, in the last years of the Napoleonic wars, to commemorate a distinctively English life, to define and celebrate the typical communal relations of a small English district. 'English verdure, English culture, English comfort'—the warmth of Emma's appraisal of the 'sweet view' of Donwell Abbey (*E* 360) may not then be just a passing notation of the character's feelings, but a key moment in the novel's thematisation of Englishness.

This focus on a single country contrasts with Austen's present-day almost world-wide reputation. Despite scholars' increasing valuation of the novels of Austen's contemporaries,

and the appearance of many of these texts in well-edited
editions, such as those from Broadview Press in Canada, despite
increasing interest in such figures as Wollstonecraft, as well as
the premiere on the West End stage of Fanny Burney's comedy
A Busy Day after two hundred years, Austen remains the only
novelist of her time whose books are still widely available and
read, whose characters' names—Lizzie Bennet, Mr Collins—
are familiar references. A volume of *Antipodean Views* for
example, has revealed that Austen is the favourite reading of
many Australian and New Zealand writers, artists and public
figures.[6] A volume of essays and a recent conference in
Bologna, 'Jane Austen Oggi e Ieri', have been entirely devoted
to her work.[7] Austen is the only British novelist of her time
whose books are taught in colleges and universities around
the world, including the European countries whose existence
she barely acknowledges. Austen is increasingly understood to
be the 'canonical' British author, who, as nineteenth century
critics often claimed, rivals Shakespeare in her naturalness
and dramatic qualities, if not in the compass and variety of
her art.

How do we account for this singular and paradoxical success
story? How does such an insular, even isolationist writer appeal
to readers and critics of quite different cultural traditions?
One answer is readily available. Austen's work coincides with
the crucial decades of British imperial consolidation. After
the final defeat of Napoleon in 1815, the stage was set for the
dramatic expansion of British influence and power throughout
the globe that was such a feature of the nineteenth century.
And with the expansion of British power went the
promulgation of British authors, and the teaching of these
authors in schools, universities, and colleges. And thus, so the
story goes, Austen enters the consciousness of subaltern and
colonised peoples. Her presence in the present day culture of
those peoples is a fall-out from the power of the empire on
which the sun never set.

There is obviously a good deal to be said for this explanation.
Many scholars as well as general readers encountered Austen's
work in those countries—Australia, Canada, the Indian

sub-continent in particular—that formerly were part of the British imperial domains. In this line of argument, Austen's insular Englishness would not be a liability but the key source of her attractiveness for educators and her charisma for readers. For, taught and propagated in alien colonial settings, Austen's restriction of interest in her novels—the very limitation of her subject-matter that commentators during the nineteenth century remarked on—becomes a missionary strength. If we conceive of Austen's novels as promoting, unconsciously or deliberately, a specifically English world—as proposing, in effect, that England *is* the world—then the appeal of her work for educators promoting 'British', or English, culture becomes clear. If her novels at best but nod to the presence of other national cultures, then so much the more useful for educators concerned to impress upon their audiences the power and hegemony of that culture. The subliminal message of Austen's work—English culture is culture—in effect dismisses other competitors from the field.

This cannot though be a complete account of Austen's present day presence on syllabuses, and screens, throughout the world. Nor can the subsidiary explanation, that this comes about because of the increasing prevalence of English as a world language, and of the dominance of American culture—into which 'Austen' has been subsumed. Translations of her novels are popular in Germany and Spain. She is read equally avidly in south America as in New Zealand. Another way of looking at Austen's Englishness in fact is to say that she presents for some readers a kind of idyll, as the American critic Lionel Trilling long ago proposed of *Emma*:[8] her work for these readers offers a space that is reassuring and comfortable, precisely because it is free of cultural conflict, free of the anxieties always called up by the recognition that one's own fundamental values and priorities might be contested. For sentimentalists, Jane Austen's England becomes, in effect, 'Jane Austen's world'—that familiar talisman invoking Regency dress, the English country house, an ideal of refined manners and genteel behaviour; a domestic or home 'world' free of disputed values, sexual ambiguity or violence. The placid assumption made by the novels that the social scene they depict is universal in effect dissolves the specificity of 'England' into a 'world'. Its implicit xenophobia seems to dissolve with it.

The scholarly interest in relating Austen to the other literature of her time is only an aspect of a much broader push to relate Austen's novels to the historical and political circumstances out of which they emerge, under the rubric of cultural materialism or new historicism. Austen's project of making a small income for herself out of novel publication, for instance, would not have been possible without the great increase in literacy in the latter part of the eighteenth century and the development of the circulating libraries which were a consequence. These in turn were a product of much increased material prosperity and the formation of the 'lady' as a distinct class and commercial market. (*The Lady's Magazine* had begun in 1775, nearly half a century behind *The Gentleman's Magazine*.) Much contemporary scholarly interest in Austen then calls back the political and social contexts that her novels appear almost to make vanish. These readings seek to repoliticize— which means in many instances to re-imperialise—novels which skilfully de-politicize their material, to bring the margins to the centre, the sides to the middle. Thus recent criticism of *Mansfield Park* has pointed to the importance to the Bertram family fortunes of the Antiguan estates from which some of their income is drawn, even though this aspect is barely mentioned in the text. Reversing the novel's own emphasis, it reads Mansfield in the light of Antigua, making 'the slave trade' about which Fanny Price ventures to question her uncle a key to the novel's treatment of gender relations. What the novel refers to in passing has become a tantalising interpretive signal for a criticism increasingly alert to its presence on the 'world stage'.[9] (A full account of these arguments is given in Chapter 7 '(De)colonising *Mansfield Park*'.)

The peripheral invocation of the British empire in *Mansfield Park* is echoed in *Persuasion*, a novel in which Austen simultaneously exposes English insularity, and, by turning it to comic account, effectively depoliticizes its implications. In *Emma*, Europe is similarly peripheral. In the very Donwell

Abbey scene in which Emma so pointedly admires the Englishness of the landscape, 'abroad' is fleetingly present among the 'engravings . . . corals, shells' with which Mr Woodhouse is amused whilst the rest of the party are outdoors. 'They were looking over views in Swisserland' (364). Frank Churchill, cross and flustered after his meeting with Jane Fairfax, petulantly declares his intention to see 'some of these places'. By contrast, in Maria Edgeworth's *Ormond* (1817) the hero, catching sight of his beloved apparently encouraging a rival suitor, starts off immediately for France. Churchill, similarly impetuous, having quarrelled with Jane at Box Hill, renews his scheme of going 'abroad for a couple of years' (373), but that is as far as it gets. Two chapters depict Harry Ormond's conquest of Parisian high society and are the occasion for a contrast—standard for the period—between French 'profligacy' and English 'domestic virtues'. (Edgeworth, for example, makes the same comparison between the English 'amiable' and the French 'aimable' as Mr Knightley (*E* 149).) [10] The difference is that Edgeworth, like almost all the other novelists of the time, sees the exotic 'abroad' as a novelistic opportunity; for Austen it is as if Europe, abroad, the extensive empire beyond the seas, is literally unimaginable.

I would argue then that the effort to turn sides to middle— to insert Europe and the empire into novels which so distinctively refuse more than minimal negotiation with these entities—counterproductive, and risks skirting or overlooking the central questions that Austen's popularity pose. This repoliticization of Austen cannot explain the power with which such novels, focused on a small area of middle-class life and aspiration, have upon contemporary readers in many parts of the globe, though this critical strategy does of course respond to the fact of Austen's status and reputation as, in some ways, a quintessentially English novelist. As I have indicated I think it is partly the absence of contestation or cultural contrast, so that the place depicted in the novels can figure imaginatively as a 'world', that is one source of this power. It is precisely Austen's ignoring of other cultures which constitutes her authority.

There are other, more crucial, explanations, which I shall briefly indicate in the final part of this essay. But first, one obvious fact should be acknowledged: apart from scholars, the overwhelming majority of Austen's readers, the members of Jane Austen societies, the audiences for films and videos, are female. An explanation for her popularity must include an explanation for this fact. I want to argue that the power of Austen's novels rests not only in their presentation of plausible 'romantic' narratives, but in their articulation, as no other texts of her time do, of the challenges faced in the formation of a self—specifically and particularly the formation of a female self. It is partly true that the novels offer models; coming to many subaltern cultures with the authority of the centre, they present images and models of girlhood and female presence already loaded with an extratextual appeal. They come furthermore with the authority of history. The moment, the historical epoch or era at which these novels depict their young ladies facing the challenges of their womanhood is one that first occurred in England. The time of the French and Napoleonic wars is one of 'unrivalled prosperity' for the landed interest,[11] resulting in much more generally diffused affluence. This moment, which can be roughly characterised as the shift from traditional to commercial society, or the modern, has been and is now, much later, replicated and repeated in other parts of the globe. In other words, Austen's novels evoke and dramatise the very moment of the emergence of the modern.

Austen's female heroines then are faced with the challenge that I have characterised as 'the formation of a self'.[12] This challenge is of course at the same time a privilege, a result of their leisure, affluence and their comparative freedom. Austen's heroines belong to a group who, perhaps for the first time in history, have the possibility of choice of sexual partner, but their choices, crucially, are constricted and partly governed by the pressures of the family that still continues, as a remnant of traditional, or pre-modern social arrangements, to have power, and that seeks to consolidate that power through its alliances. In other words, the dream of individual choice remains in tension with the economic and dynastic ambitions of the family—as most dramatically exemplified in *Mansfield*

Park. In the historical world of Austen's novels, as in many parts of the world today, except in the 'developed' West, to choose a sexual partner is inevitably to choose a marriage partner. Moreover, in many parts of the world, the family arranges the marriage, and the girl declines the partner chosen for her at great risk. Whilst this is not precisely the situation in any of Austen's novels, their depiction of the social and economic pressures driving women towards a prudent, rather than a romantic, choice makes them closely approximate this condition. Marriage is crucial to the action of Austen's novels, as of her contemporaries, because in this single event are focused both the personal issues that modernity foregrounds and the dynastic relations of the still continuing pre-modern arrangements.

In a fascinating article about the teaching of *Mansfield Park* in an elite college in Delhi, Ruth Vanita has shown how her students both identified with, and dis-identified with, the novel's heroine, the quiet, submissive Fanny Price.[13] As Vanita writes, the students recognised in the heroine's situation many of the lineaments of their own position. As girls they are denied privileges accorded to their brothers, for instance, just as Fanny is denied the privileges given to her cousins. But the students disliked what one might call Fanny's coping style—her quiet dutifulness, her need to make herself valued by being 'good'. Vanita stresses how reluctant her female students were to recognise Fanny's courage in resisting the family's concerted attempt to make her marry Henry Crawford. Most interestingly, she suggests that the contempt some students expressed for Fanny was really self-contempt at a female role many were in reality forced to adopt in modern Indian society.

These reactions, however, are found also in Australian students, whose social situation is not at all similar to their Indian counterparts. Anglo-Saxon Australian (and 'assimilated') girls are generally free to choose their sexual partners— or at least this is the prevailing cultural assumption—and they are not generally treated as inferior to their male peers. They, too, despise Fanny Price. Hers is a life governed by constrictions and denials, and many young readers do not want to imaginatively align themselves with such a life, or do not allow themselves to understand how little free in effect a life may be. One cannot help thinking, though, that if the truth were told, many of these students—quiet, intelligent girls, whose inner life is sustained by reading—resemble Fanny far more than they do Elizabeth Bennet.

What this suggests is how compellingly still the novels represent models of the female self—how compellingly they suggest possible alternatives, and how effective and substantial is their representation of the constricting setting in which that self must be formed. Hence Charlotte Lucas's decision to marry Mr Collins in *Pride and Prejudice* remains a controversial site of discussion for almost all readers. 'The whole family, in short', relates the narrator, 'were properly overjoyed on the occasion. The younger girls formed hopes of coming out a year or two sooner than they might have done; and the boys were relieved from their apprehension of Charlotte's dying an old maid. Charlotte herself was tolerably composed' (*P* 122). There has been no direct pressure from her family; nevertheless Charlotte's practice in this crucial passage of her life cannot be thought of outside the circumstances formed by her family and financial position. Rather than bending to social demands, though, Charlotte—it might well be argued— has made her best deal. Taking everything into account, she has done the best for herself, and if this involves a life with a man she does not, and cannot, love, so be it. The novelist's fiercely ironic tones in this passage condemn Charlotte's decision, but not all readers are swayed by them. And the novel itself seems to back-track on its earlier verdict, seeing that Charlotte manages things well, and implicitly, perhaps, criticising Elizabeth's youthful, outright condemnation. The reader is required to both feel and share Elizabeth's moral outrage, and to recognise the real force of the commonplace circumstances that dictate Charlotte's actions: a tension that results in the continuing debate about whether Charlotte was 'right' to do what she did. To hold out for 'a handsome, amiable, unexceptionable Young Man (such as do not much abound in real Life)', as Austen remarks wryly in a letter (277) is not always possible.

Many novels of the era feature heroines whose choice of partner runs up against the disapproval of parents or guardians—Burney's *Cecilia* (1782), for instance. The novel of sentiment had encouraged the representation of a character's internal narrative, their often disturbed or conflicted thoughts and feelings, and often represented these as a private 'soliloquy'. Neither of these aspects then can wholly account for Austen's salience and power to involve contemporary readers. What makes Austen's work unique is that the process of self-formation I have singled out—which Austen conceives of as an ongoing sequence or cascade of moral decisions, minor and major—is both observed, and participated in, by the reader. I will comment briefly on three aspects of this crucial dynamic of the novels. It is partly achieved by the narrative innovation which is clumsily called 'free indirect speech' or 'discourse'. Austen's presentation of her heroine's thoughts allows us at one and the same time access to these as private and absolute, and an awareness—or potential awareness—of their contingency or folly. It allows us to be both inside and outside, present with, and alert to the future of, the figure, both serious and amused. Thus narratively, the novels animate the simultaneous freedom and imagined 'autonomy' of the heroine, and the historical or social setting which curtails and governs that freedom. Mid-twentieth century critics thought of the process within the novels as education, and they were partly right: the novels present us with a gradual filling in of the heroine's interior space that is simultaneously her acculturation. Austen's innovation is that acculturation occurs in tandem with the making of a self present to itself. Cultural materialist critics often present this as a process of Althusserian 'interpellation' of a subject-reader largely passively conceived;[14] I prefer to stress the degree to which these texts invite the reader's collaboration in a process that is indistinguishable from the active generation of a 'self'.

A second aspect of this innovation, as Deidre Lynch has argued, is the novel's predication upon re-reading. Austen's novels present the reader with many examples of re-reading and re-thinking, from Elizabeth Bennet's revision of Darcy in front of his portrait, to the conversations of Fanny Price and Edmund Bertram in which the reader, with them, reappraises the character of Mary Crawford, to the conversation in Chapter 5 of *Emma* in which the figure to whom we have been introduced is discussed by her friends, Mr Knightley and Mrs Weston, to Anne Elliot's wholesale reappraisal of her past on which the action of *Persuasion* is founded. But these exemplary instances of re-reading are less significant than the dynamic process whereby the reader herself is made to re-read. Austen presents Darcy's letter in one chapter, without comment, and the reader reads it. In the next, passages of the letter are requoted, as Elizabeth re-reads them, and her thoughts are dramatised; by the end of this process, the reader, like the character, has perused the letter at least twice, knows the letter almost by heart, and revised their initial opinions. *Emma* famously invites re-reading, and repeated re-reading, to be appreciated and understood. By taking the reading consciousness through a process of revision and revisal, Lynch argues, Austen distinguished her novels from the common novel 'trash' of the day, and put her readers in a privileged position.[15]

One-third means by which Austen fosters the reader's own collaboration with the moral dynamic of the novels is through her comedy. Earlier critics have shown how Austen, following Burney's *Evelina*, demonstrates the conjunction of bad taste and moral failure in her 'vulgar' characters like the Thorpes or Mrs Elton. The characteristic comic techniques of exposing such characters' contradictions (Mrs Elton's speech about strawberries at Donwell Abbey is a good example), or the disparity between their pretentious speech and their actual behaviour, often elicits the reader's amusement. Such procedures in the texts do not simply persuade the reader into a superior (ironic or satiric) position. They require, like the reading of free indirect speech, and the revision of the narrative, the reader's active collaboration. To 'get' or to see a joke is to distinguish one's inner life from the life of the object perceived as comic, even if, or perhaps especially if, a certain amount of 'identification' is present in the mixture. (See Chapter 5 'Mrs Bennet's Least Favourite Daughter'.) In such modes the process of education in the novels, the process I have called 'self-formation', becomes an active transference to the reader.

The reader of Austen then is formed into a reflective self. This enhancement of interiority is the source, I believe, of Austen's success with readers of our time. The social and historical position of many women around the globe resembles that of women of Austen's period,[16] but even when that is not the case, the process of self-formation is so crucial to the project of individualism on which modernity and post-modernity are founded, that these novels in which that project was first exemplified and demonstrated, and the constraints of the family in which it is played out, remain tellingly contemporary. But the process of self-formation exemplified by Austen's heroines is only part of what makes Austen's novels such an important, even necessary part of the contemporary reader's own self-formation.

'Jane Austen's world', then, is for some readers a faux England that never did, and never could, exist. But the continuing popularity of her work, and its continuing and even increasing academic prestige, rests fundamentally upon her art. This art has many aspects, only some of which I have glanced at here. But in this context, it is an art which simultaneously acknowledges an abroad, an empire, outside the site of the text, and declines to have much to do with it. Instead it directs its focus, and the reader's energies, upon the creation of an interior life of the self, that interior life which is not the birthright but the prize of modernity. Austen's England is then, in effect, the contemporary world.

Notes

MRS BENNET'S LEAST FAVOURITE DAUGHTER

1. Roger Gard, *Jane Austen's Art of Clarity*, New Haven and London: Yale University Press, 1993, p. 99.
2. This is the argument of the chapter on the novel in my *Recreating Jane Austen*, Cambridge: Cambridge University Press, 2002.
3. Slavoj Zizek, *The Obscure Object of Ideology*, London and New York: Verso, 1989, p. 64.
4. Julia Prewitt Brown, *Jane Austen's Novels: Social Change and Literary Form*, Cambridge Mass.: Harvard University Press, 1979, p. 66.
5. D.W. Harding, 'Character and Caricature in Jane Austen' in *Regulated Hatred and Other Essays on Jane Austen*, London: Athlone Press, 1998, p. 99.
6. Deirdre Le Faye (ed.), *Jane Austen's Letters*, 3rd edn., Oxford: Oxford University Press, 1995, p. 202.
7. Puff: 'The pruning knife—zounds! The axe! Why, here has been such lopping and topping, I shan't have the bare trunk of my play left presently!' Jane Austen refers to 'Mr Sheridan's play of The Critic' in 'The History of England', in R.W. Chapman (ed.), *The Oxford Illustrated Jane Austen*, Vol. VI, *Minor Works*, p. 148.
8. The recent books by Paula Byrne and Penny Gay have made this indubitable (Paula Byrne, *Jane Austen and the Theatre*, London: Hambledon and London, 2002; Penny Gay, *Jane Austen and the Theatre*, Cambridge: Cambridge University Press, 2002).
9. Tara Ghoshal Wallace, *Jane Austen and Narrative Authority*, London and New York: St Martin's Press, 1995, p. 46.
10. Thomas R. Edwards, 'Embarrassed by Jane Austen', *Raritan*, 7:1, 1987, pp. 62–80, 73.
11. Using the term made current by Deleuze and Guattari, William C. Dowling describes Mrs Bennet and figures like her in Austen as 'desiring machines'—'the scandal from which one wants to

avert one's eyes is that of a human creature that has chosen to live out its life at the level of blind drives'. *Evelina* and the Geneology of Literary Shame, *Eighteenth-Century Life*, 16 November 1992, pp. 208–220, 212.

12. She resembles Mrs Norris in this: Edwards speaks of 'her demented yearning to govern and in effect *live* other people's lives' (p. 75).

13. See Paula Bennett, 'Family Plots: *Pride and Prejudice* as a novel about parenting', in *Approaches to Teaching Austen's* Pride and Prejudice, Marcia McClintock Folsom (ed.), MLA 1993.

EDITING *MANSFIELD PARK*

1. David Gilson, *A Bibliography of Jane Austen*, 2nd edn., St Paul's Bibliographies, Winchester, 1997, p. 60.

2. Claudia L. Johnson (ed.), *Mansfield Park: Authoritative Text, Contexts, Criticism*, New York: Norton, 1998, p. 324.

3. Philip Gaskell, *A New Introduction to Bibliography*, Oxford: Clarendon, 1974, pp. 112, 352.

4. 'The mere Trash of the common Circulating Library, I hold in the highest contempt,' declares Sir Edward Denham in *Sanditon*, in R.W. Chapman (ed.), *The Oxford Illustrated Jane Austen*, Vol. VI, *Minor Works*, p. 403.

5. Figures range from the £50 said to be paid per volume by Longman (Jan Fergus, *Jane Austen, a Literary Life*, London: Macmillan, 1991, p. 15) to the much smaller sums mentioned in the chapter 'Professional Women Novelists: Earning an Income', in Cheryl Turner, *Living By the Pen: Women Writers in the Eighteenth Century*, London and New York: Routledge, 1992, pp. 102–116, though there is evidence fees increased in the nineteenth century.

6. Lee Erickson, *The Economy of Literary Form: English Literature and the Industrialization of Publishing 1800–1850*, Baltimore and London: Johns Hopkins University Press, 1996, p. 133. Erikson cites Robert Southey's *Letters from England* (1809): 'It is not a mere antithesis to say that they who buy books do not read them, and that they who do read them do not buy them.'

7. Sarah Harriet Burney, an author herself, owned a copy of *Mansfield Park*, and she was not rich. But she may have bought it at the later discounted price. Other owners included Madame de Staël and the Duchess of Wellington (Gilson, 52–54).

8. Deirdre Le Faye (ed.), *Jane Austen's Letters*, 3rd edn., Oxford University Press, 1995, p. 287.

9. See Jan Fergus, *Jane Austen: A Literary Life*, London: Macmillan, 1991, pp. 190–92, n. 47.

10. William Austen-Leigh and Richard Arthur Austen-Leigh, revised and enlarged by Deidre Le Faye, *Jane Austen: A Family Record*, London: The British Library, 1989, p.198.

11. Deirdre Le Faye, *Letters*, op. cit., p. 291. Le Faye's note (p. 445) refers to Samuel Bagstock, another bookseller/publisher, who tells a story that turns on a missed appointment, and a message saying 'Finding you out, I decline your offer.' According to Bagstock, Murray then bursts in whilst the family are at dinner, saying 'Pray Sir! What have you found me out in doing?' (*Samuel Bagster of London, 1772–1851, An Autobiography*, London: Samuel Bagster & Sons Ltd, 1972, pp. 168–69). Is this evidence of roguery? When Murray arranged for Scott to review *Emma* in the *Quarterly* he was doing Austen a good turn, as Fergus notes (p. 158) since he stood to gain very little himself from the success of a novel published on commission.

12. Deirdre Le Faye, *Jane Austen: A Family Record*, London: The British Library, 1989, p. 202.

13. Hilda M. Hamlyn, 'Eighteenth-Century Circulating Libraries in England', *The Library*, Series 5, Vol. I, 1947, p. 219.

14. See John Guillory, *Cultural Capital: The Problem of Literary Canon Formation*, Chicago and London: University of Chicago Press, 1993. Guillory argues that 'it is only by understanding the social function and institutional protocols of the school that we will understand how works are preserved, reproduced, and disseminated over successive generations and centuries' (vii). I would argue that publishers such as Murray and Bentley were at least as important as the academy in constituting something like a list of classics or standard works, and disseminating that understanding.

15. Analysing the scenes of re-reading in *Pride and Prejudice* (Elizabeth reviewing Darcy's letter, revisiting his portrait) Deidre Shauna Lynch argues that this 'is typical of the fictions that mediated the experience of the expanded book market: Austen identifies to her readers the proper means of and motives for literary experience when she demonstrates that the truth of a letter is situated beyond or beneath the page and when she demonstrates that character cannot be known at first sight.' By insisting on the necessity of re-reading (and by devising means which force

the reader to undergo the process of re-reading) Austen, in Lynch's argument, enforces the distinction between her, incipiently 'literary' or canonical, text and the mass market. Re-reading is crucial to the canonical novel's inculcation of interiority and reflection in its readers. Deidre Shauna Lynch, *The Economy of Character; novels, market culture, and the business of inner meaning*, Chicago: University of Chicago Press, 1998, pp. 131, 130–132.

16. Deirdre Le Faye, *Letters*, op. cit., pp. 201, 203.
17. 'Introductory Note', p. xii, in *Mansfield Park*, R.W. Chapman (ed.), Oxford: Clarendon Press, [1923], 1946.
18. Deirdre Le Faye, *Letters*, op. cit., p. 300.
19. The printer of the second volume, C. Roworth, was the same for both publishers: in resetting the volume for Murray he follows his earlier work pretty closely.
20. Kathryn Sutherland (ed.), *Mansfield Park*, Harmondsworth: Penguin, 1996.
21. Kathryn Sutherland, 'Speaking Commas/Reading Commas: Punctuating *Mansfield Park*', *Text*, 12, 1999, p. 115.
22. 'Note on the Text', p. xliii in Sutherland (ed.), *Mansfield Park*, op. cit., 1996.

(DE)COLONISING *MANSFIELD PARK*

1. Edward W. Said, *Culture and Imperialism*, London: Vintage, 1994, pp. 95–115. See also R.S. Neale, 'Zapp Zapped: Property and Alienation in *Mansfield Park*', in *Writing Marxist History, British Society, Economy and Culture since 1700*, Oxford: Basil Blackwell, 1985, pp. 87–108. Sir Thomas and slavery is discussed in Avrom Fleishman, *A Reading of Mansfield Park* (1967), Baltimore: Johns Hopkins University Press, 1970, pp. 36–39. Other accounts will be mentioned in the course of this chapter.
2. Susan Fraiman, 'Jane Austen and Edward Said: Gender, Culture and Imperialism' in Deidre Lynch (ed.), *Janeites: Austen's Disciples and Devotees*, Princeton and Oxford: Princeton University Press, 2000, pp. 206–223, 206.
3. Claudia L. Johnson (ed.), *Mansfield Park, Authoritative Text, Contexts, Criticism*, New York: Norton, 1998. The essays are Said's, Brian Southam's 'The Silence of the Bertrams', and Joseph Lew's '"That Abominable Traffic"; *Mansfield Park* and the Dynamics of Slavery'.
4. Katie Trumpener, 'The Virago Jane Austen' in Deidre Lynch

(ed.), *Janeites: Austen's Disciples and Devotees*, Princeton and Oxford: Princeton University Press, 2000, pp. 140–165, 154.

5. The video is marketed (in Australia at least) as 'A film by Patricia Rozema': Austen's name is not mentioned.

6. Joseph Lew, '"That Abominable Traffic": *Mansfield Park* and the Dynamics of Slavery', in Beth Fowkles Tobin (ed.), *History, Gender and Eighteenth Century Literature*, Athens: University of Georgia Press, 1994, pp. 271–300.

7. June Sturrock (ed.), *Mansfield Park*, Peterborough, Ontario: Broadview Press, 2001, p. 23.

8. Peter Smith, '*Mansfield Park* and the World Stage', *The Cambridge Quarterly*, 23, 3, 1994, pp. 203–229, 207.

9. Fraiman, 'Jane Austen and Edward Said', op. cit., pp. 206-223, 212.

10. Moira Ferguson, '*Mansfield Park*, Slavery, Colonialism and Gender', *Oxford Literary Review*, 3, 1991, pp. 118–139, 128.

11. A postcolonial reading more sympathetic to the figure is given in Katie Trumpener, *Bardic Nationalism: the Romantic Novel and the British Empire*, Princeton: University Press, 1997.

12. Trevor Lloyd, 'Myths of the Indies: Jane Austen and the British Empire', *Comparative Criticism*, 21, 1999, pp. 50–78. Like other critics considered later in this essay, Lloyd hypothesises about Sir Thomas's activities in Antigua and assembles evidence to suggest that the purpose of his visit was to sell the estate.

13. Brian Southam, 'The Silence of the Bertrams, Slavery and the chronology of *Mansfield Park*', *TLS*, 17 February 1995, pp. 13–14.

14. Margaret Kirkham, *Jane Austen, Feminism and Fiction*, Harvester Wheatsheaf, 1983, pp. 116–119.

15. G.B. Hill and L.F. Powell (eds.), *Boswell's Life of Johnson*, Oxford: Clarendon Press, 1934, Vol. III, p. 87.

16. Fraser Easton, for example, points out that Mansfield was 'a key legislative supporter of economic modernization'; 'The political economy of *Mansfield Park*: Fanny Price and the Atlantic working class', *Textual Practice*, 12, 3, 1998, pp. 459–88, 460.

17. This connection was first noted by Joseph Wiesenfarth, in *The Errand of Form*, New York: Fordham University Press, 1967, p. 90.

18. Jocelyn Harris, *Jane Austen's Art of Memory*, Cambridge: Cambridge University Press, p. 137 'Mrs Norris is well-named as the bad nurse': Barbara Hardy, 'The objects in *Mansfield Park*', John Halperin (ed.), *Bicentenary Essays*, Cambridge: Cambridge University Press, 1975, p. 185.

19. Carl Plasa, '"What was done there is not to be told": *Mansfield Park*'s Colonial Unconscious', *Textual Politics from Slavery to Postcolonialism*, London and New York: Routledge, 2001, pp. 32–59, 35.

20. Ferguson, '*Mansfield Park*, Slavery, Colonialism and Gender', op. cit., p. 121.

21. Barbara K. Seeber, *General Consent in Jane Austen: A study of dialogism*, Montreal and Kingston: McGill-Queen's University Press, 2000, p. 97.

22. Said, *Culture and Imperialism*, op. cit., p. 104, p. 106. In these and the following quotations the italics are mine.

23. Ferguson, '*Mansfield Park*, Slavery, Colonialism and Gender', op. cit., p. 121.

24. Plasa 'Colonial Unconscious', op. cit., p. 35.

25. Clara Tuite, 'Domestic retrenchment and imperial expansion: the property plots of *Mansfield Park*', in You-me Park and Rajeswari Sunder Rajan (eds.), *The Postcolonial Austen*, London and New York: Routledge, 2000, pp. 93–115, 93.

26. Ibid., p. 109.

27. Deidre Coleman, 'Conspicuous Consumption: White Abolitionism and English Women's Protest Writing in the 1790s', ELH, 61 (1994), pp. 341–362.

28. Quoted by Lew, 'Abominable Traffic', op. cit., p. 277.

29. 'The White Slave Trade, hints towards forming a bill for the Abolition of the White Female Slave Trade, in the Cities of London and Westminster, *The Weekly Entertainer or agreeable and instructive repository*, 45, Sherborne, Monday 12 August 1805. Robert Hole, *Selected Writings of Hannah More*, London; William Pickering, 1996, pp. 36–41, 39.

30. Quoted by John Wiltshire, *Jane Austen and the Body*, Cambridge: Cambridge University Press, 1992, pp. 100–101.

31. In Douglas Hall (ed.), *Miserable Slavery, Thomas Thistlewood in Jamaica 1750-86*, Macmillan, 1989, pp. 88–9, 95, for example.

32. Quoted in Elsa V. Goveia, *Slave Society in the British Leeward Islands at the End of the Eighteenth Century*, [1965], Westport: Connecticut: Greenwood Press, 1980, p. 135.

33. Lew, 'Abonimable Traffic', op. cit., p. 290.

34. Another Maria, in Edgeworth's *Patronage*, published the same year as *Mansfield Park* (1814) is a useful parallel case. 'Maria Hauton shall be married this day fortnight', declares Lord Oldborough, in furtherance of his political ambitions. 'Maria Hauton was sent for to her uncle's study, heard her doom in

sullen silence, but she made no show of resistance, and Lord Oldborough was satisfied.' (p. 103, Pandora Press edition, 1986.) Like Maria Bertram, Maria Hauton is in love with another man, but she effectively disappears from the text at this point, a mere item in a system of exchange.

35. This general point is implied in Aijaz Ahmad, *In Theory; Classes, Nations, Literatures,* London and New York: Verso, 1992, p. 186.

36. As bell hooks argues in 'Racism and Feminism'; *'Ain't I a Woman: Black Women and Feminism,* Boston: South End Press, 1981, p. 144.

37. Lew, 'Abominable Traffic', op. cit., p. 279.

38. Ferguson, '*Mansfield Park,* Slavery, Colonialism and Gender', op. cit., p. 126.

39. Southam, 'The Silence of the Bertrams', op. cit., p. 14.

40. Were this line of argument to have any validity, one might note that 'the town and also the county of Northampton' offers support to the abolitionists as early as 1788: Thomas Clarkson, *The History of the Abolition of the African Slave Trade,* [1808], Reprinted London: Frank Cass, 1968, Vol. I, p. 468.

41. Mary Brunton, *Discipline,* London: Pandora Press, 1986, p. 117.

42. Ruth Perry, 'Austen and Empire: A Thinking Woman's Guide to British Imperialism', *Persuasions,* 16, 1994, pp. 95–106, 103.

43. Tom Gibbon, 'The Antiguan Connection', *The Cambridge Quarterly,* 11, 1982, pp. 298–305.

44. Deirdre Le Faye (ed.), op. cit., *Letters,* p. 198 (24th January 1813).

45. Perry (*Austen and Empire,* op. cit., p. 97) gives a list: her brother James' father-in-law, for example.

46. Clarkson, *Abolition of the African Slave Trade,* op. cit., Vol. II, p. 228.

47. Ibid., p. 552.

48. Edwards, *History,* Vol. II, 40, quoted by Goveia, op. cit., p. 24.

49. Gideon Polya, *Jane Austen and the Black Hole of British History,* privately published, Melbourne, 1998.

50. Simon Schama, *Rembrandt's Eyes,* London: Allen Lane, The Penguin Press, 1999.

51. See Jon Mee, 'Austen's Treacherous Ivory' in *The Postcolonial Austen,* edited by You-me Park and Rajeswari Sunder Rajan, London and New York: Routledge, 2001, pp. 74–92.

52. 'Jane Austen at Sixty', *Nation and Athenaeum,* 34, 1923, pp. 433–4.

53. Clara Tuite, 'Domestic Retrenchment', op. cit., pp. 93–115.

54. Southam, 'The Silence of the Bertrams', op. cit., p. 14.

55. Plasa, 'Colonial Unconscious', op. cit., p. 36.

56. Ferguson, '*Mansfield Park*, Slavery, Colonialism and Gender', op. cit., p. 133.

57. Kathryn Sutherland, Introduction to *Mansfield Park*, Harmondsworth: Penguin, 1996, p.xvii.

58. Mary Favret, 'Free and Happy: Jane Austen in America', *Janeites: Austen's Disciples and Devotees*, Deidre Lynch ed., Princeton and Oxford: Princeton University Press, 2000, pp. 166–187, 179.

59. Tuite, op. cit.

60. Perry, 'Austen and Empire', op. cit., p. 104

61. Milan Kundera, *Testaments Betrayed, An essay in Nine Parts*, New York: Harper Collins, 1995.

COMFORT, HEALTH AND CREATIVITY: A READING OF *EMMA*

1. Oliver Sacks, *A Leg to Stand On*, London: Picador, 1985, p. 125.

2. See Chapter 5, 'Ease' in Witold Rybczynski, *Home: A short history of an idea*, New York: Viking Penguin, 1986, pp. 101–121, especially, pp. 120–121.

3. Letter to Francis Austen, 26 July 1809.

4. Joy Alexander counts at least 129 occurrences of comfort or its derivatives in *Mansfield Park*. She shows how in that novel the word ranges in meaning from 'being cossetted' to the older sense of 'being strengthened and consoled', with Fanny Price filling the role of the Comforter; Joy Alexander, 'Anything Goes? Reading *Mansfield Park*', *The Use of English*, 52, 3, 2001, pp. 239–51.

5. 'No fresh air, no blue hill, no bonny beck. I should hardly like to live with her ladies and gentlemen, in their elegant but confined houses', Letter to G.H. Lewes, 12 January 1848; 'she ruffles her reader by nothing vehement, disturbs him by nothing profound'. Letter to W.S. Williams, 12 April 1850: etc.

JANE AUSTEN'S ENGLAND, JANE AUSTEN'S WORLD

1. Deirdre Le Faye (ed.), *Letters*, op. cit., pp. 323, 275.

2. Franco Moretti, *Atlas of the European Novel*, London: Verso, 1998, provides illuminating maps to illustrate this point.

3. Katie Trumpener, *Bardic Nationalism: the Romantic Novel and the British Empire*, Princeton: University Press, 1997, p. 297, n. 45.

4. Maggie Lane, *Jane Austen's England*, London: Robert Hale, 1986.
5. Linda Colley, *Britons: Forging the Nation 1707–1837*, New Haven and London: Yale University Press, 1992, p. 273, and *passim.*
6. Susannah Fullerton and Anne Harbers, eds., *Jane Austen: Antipodean Views*, Sydney: Wellington Lane Press, 2001.
7. See Beatrice Battaglia (ed.), *Jane Austen Oggi e Ieri*, Ravenna: Longo, 2002.
8. '*Emma* and the Legend of Jane Austen' [1957] in Trilling, *Beyond Culture*, Harmondsworth: Peregrine, 1967, pp. 42–61.
9. Smith, Peter, '*Mansfield Park* and the World Stage', *Cambridge Quarterly*, 23, 3, 1994, pp. 203–229. The most influential text here is Edward W. Said, *Culture and Imperialism*, etc. Recent contributions elaborating Said's work include Clara Tuite and Carl Plasa.
10. Maria Edgeworth, *Ormond* in *Harrington and Ormond*, Vol. III, pp. 192, 267.
11. Colley, *Britons*, op. cit., p. 158.
12. Trilling makes a similar observation when he suggests that 'Jane Austen, conservative and even conventional as she was, perceived the nature of the deep psychological change which accompanied the establishment of democratic society . . . she understood the new necessity of conscious self-definition and self-criticism.' (*Beyond Culture*, op. cit., p. 54)
13. Ruth Vanita, '*Mansfield Park* in Miranda House', in Rajeswari Sunder Rajan (ed.), *The Lie of the Land: English Literary Studies in India*, Delhi: Oxford University Press, 1993, pp. 90–98.
14. See for example, Lisa Lowe, 'Decolonisation, Displace-ment, Disidentification; Asian-American "novels" and the Question of History', in Deidre Lynch and William B. Warner (eds.), *Cultural Institutions of the Novel*, Durham and London: Duke University Press, 1996. pp. 96–128, 96–98.
15. Deidre Shauna Lynch, *The Economy of Character, Novels, Market Culture and the Business of Inner Meaning*, Chicago: University Press, 1998, pp. 130–133.
16. 'Jane Austen in the Classroom: Some Indian Responses' in Harish Trivedi (ed.), *Jane Austen: An Anthology of Recent Criticism*, Delhi: Pencraft International, 1996, pp. 239–253.

Index